# Space

Reader's Digest
## Pathfinders

A Reader's Digest Pathfinder

Reader's Digest Children's Books are published by
Reader's Digest Children's Publishing, Inc.
Reader's Digest Road, Pleasantville, NY, 10570-7000, U.S.A.

Visit our web site: www.readersdigestkids.com

Conceived and produced by Weldon Owen Pty Limited
59 Victoria Street, McMahons Point, NSW, 2060, Australia
A member of the Weldon Owen Group of Companies
Sydney • San Francisco

© 1999 Weldon Owen Inc.

READER'S DIGEST CHILDREN'S PUBLISHING, INC.
General Manager: Vivian Antonangeli
Group Publisher: Rosanna Hansen
Editorial Director: Linda Falken
Senior Project Editors: Sherry Gerstein, Beverly Larson
Project Creative Director: Candy Warren
Art Director: Fredric Winkowski
Production Coordinator: Debbie Gagnon
Director of Sales and Marketing: Rosanne McManus
Director of U.S. Sales: Lola Valenciano
Marketing Director: Karen Herman

WELDON OWEN PTY LTD
Chairman: John Owen
Publisher: Sheena Coupe
Associate Publisher: Lynn Humphries
Art Director: Sue Burk
Consultant, Design Concept and Cover Design: John Bull
Design Concept: Clare Forte, Robyn Latimer
Editorial Assistants: Sarah Anderson, Trudie Craig
Production Manager: Caroline Webber
Production Assistant: Kylie Lawson
Vice President International Sales: Stuart Laurence

Author: Alan Dyer
Consultant: Roy A. Gallant
Project Editor: Jenni Bruce
Designer: Cliff Watt
Picture Research: Annette Crueger

Illustrators: Julian Baum/Wildlife Art Ltd, Tom Connell/Wildlife Art Ltd, Christer Eriksson, Murray Frederick, Chris Forsey, Lee Gibbons/Wildlife Art Ltd, Ray Grinaway, David A. Hardy/Wildlife Art Ltd, Oliver Rennert, Chris Stead, Marco Sparaciari, Tony Wellington, Rod Westblade

Library of Congress Cataloging–in–Publication Data

Dyer, A. (Alan)
Space / [Alan Dyer, author].
p.   cm. — (Reader's Digest pathfinders)
Includes index.
Summary: Examines the nature of outer space, our solar system, and our universe, including descriptions of the sun, moon, and planets, as well as constellations, nebulas and black holes.
ISBN 1-57584-291-2 (hard cover). — ISBN 1-57584-299-8 (lib. ed.)
1. Outer space—Juvenile literature.
2. Solar system—Juvenile literature. 3. Astronomy—Juvenile literature.
[1. Outer space. 2. Solar system. 3. Astronomy] I. Title.  II. Series.
QB500.22.D94   1999   520—dc21   98-53123

Color Reproduction by Colourscan Co Pte Ltd
Printed by Tien Wah Press Pte Ltd
Printed in Singapore

A WELDON OWEN PRODUCTION

# Reader's Digest
## Pathfinders

# Space

**Reader's Digest**
**Children's Books™**

Pleasantville, New York • Montréal, Québec

# Contents

# Exploring Space 6

Our Place in Space . . . . . . . . . . . . . 8
Scoping Out Space . . . . . . . . . . . . 10
Blast Off! . . . . . . . . . . . . . . . . . 12
Working in Space . . . . . . . . . . . . . 14
Robot Probes . . . . . . . . . . . . . . . . 16
Looking for Life . . . . . . . . . . . . . . 18

# Our Solar System 20

The Sun's Family . . . . . . . . . . . . . 22
Our Planet Earth . . . . . . . . . . . . . 24
Our Moon . . . . . . . . . . . . . . . . . 26
The Sun . . . . . . . . . . . . . . . . . . 28
Mercury and Venus . . . . . . . . . . . . 30
Mars . . . . . . . . . . . . . . . . . . . . 32
Asteroids and Meteoroids . . . . . . . 34
Jupiter . . . . . . . . . . . . . . . . . . . 36
Saturn . . . . . . . . . . . . . . . . . . . 38
Uranus and Neptune . . . . . . . . . . 40
Pluto and Beyond . . . . . . . . . . . . 42
Comets . . . . . . . . . . . . . . . . . . . 44

# Our Universe 46

Constellations . . . . . . . . . . . . . . . 48
Shining Stars . . . . . . . . . . . . . . . 50
Changing Stars . . . . . . . . . . . . . . 52
Nebulas . . . . . . . . . . . . . . . . . . 54
Our Galaxy . . . . . . . . . . . . . . . . 56
Galaxies and Black Holes . . . . . . . . 58
The Expanding Universe . . . . . . . . . 60

Glossary . . . . . . . . . . . . . . . . . . 62
Index . . . . . . . . . . . . . . . . . . . . 64

# Pick Your Path!

YOU ARE ABOUT to blast off on an incredible journey into *Space*. No other book offers so many paths to explore the universe. You can start out in your own cosmic neighborhood, zoom through outer space, and end in the far reaches of the universe. Or you can follow your own interests. If you're especially interested in supernovas, nature's most powerful explosions, head straight to "Changing Stars," and move through the book from there.

You'll find plenty of other discovery paths to choose from in the special features sections. Read about real-life space heroes in "Inside Story," or get creative with "Hands On" activities. Delve into words with "Word Builders," or amaze your friends with fascinating facts from "That's Amazing!" You can choose a new path with every reading—READER'S DIGEST PATHFINDERS will take you wherever *you* want to go.

## INSIDE STORY

### Space Heroes

Peer at the Milky Way with Galileo and be the first person to see the stars through a telescope. Hear the noise and feel the cockpit shake with commander Eileen Collins as the space shuttle blasts off. Study an amazing photograph with Clyde Tombaugh and discover Planet X—mysterious Pluto. INSIDE STORY introduces you to the men and women who are exploring the frontiers of space. Imagine you are there with them, and you will understand how it feels to unravel the mysteries of the universe.

## HANDS ON

### Create and Make

Use Popsicle sticks to prove Earth spins. Track the movements of Jupiter's four largest moons with binoculars. Find out when to see meteor showers. Prove for yourself why stars twinkle. Create an "alien" that might live on one of Saturn's moons. The HANDS ON features suggest experiments, projects, and activities that make astronomy—and the night sky—come alive!

### Word Builders

What a strange word! What does it mean? Where did it come from? Find out by reading **Word Builders**.

### That's Amazing!

Awesome facts, amazing records, fascinating figures—you'll find them all in **That's Amazing!**

### Pathfinder

Use the **Pathfinder** section to find your way from one subject to another. It's all up to you.

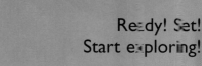

Ready! Set! Start exploring!

# Exploring Space

GET READY TO explore the mysteries of space. Your journey begins with Earth and its place in the vast universe. You then share the vision of all the people who have investigated the night sky—from early astronomers with their simple telescopes to modern scientists who capture magnificent images with the Hubble Space Telescope. Leave Earth behind and join the astronauts as they travel to the Moon aboard Apollo or orbit our planet in the space shuttle. Go where no human can go, by tracking the progress of robot probes. And ponder one of the greatest mysteries—is there other life in the universe?

page **8**

Where does Earth fit into the universe?

What are the dots in this photograph?

Go to **OUR PLACE IN SPACE.**

page **10**

Who was the first person to look at the night sky through a telescope?

What sort of radiation does just-popped toast send out?

Go to **SCOPING OUT SPACE.**

page **12**

Why does the space shuttle discard its fuel tank?

What is this astronaut doing on the Moon?

Go to **BLAST OFF!**

page **14** Where will the International Space Station be built?

How does a shuttle astronaut keep cool in space?

Go to **WORKING IN SPACE**.

page **16** How will a probe land on Titan, one of Saturn's moons?

What did the Sojourner rover find on Mars?

Go to **ROBOT PROBES**.

page **18** What sort of planet might these aliens live on?

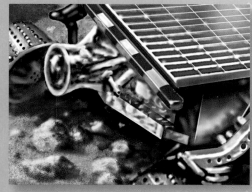

Which world's ocean might contain life?

Go to **LOOKING FOR LIFE**.

*Venus, the nearest planet*    *Andromeda, the nearest large galaxy*

**Our Planet and Its Moon**
Light-travel time to Moon =
1.3 seconds

*People have traveled only
as far as the Moon.*

# Our Place in Space

IF YOU WALK outside at night and look up at the stars, it might seem as if you are the center of the universe— surrounded by planets and stars that are moving around Earth. For thousands of years, people did think that the universe revolved around Earth.

In 1543, astronomer Nicolaus Copernicus realized that the best way to explain the motions of the planets was to say that all the planets, including Earth, moved around the Sun. Over the next century or so, the picture of the universe changed from an Earth-centered model to one with the Sun at its center. Since then, this model of the universe has grown many times. Astronomers have discovered that the Sun is just one of many stars, that it orbits far from the center of the Milky Way galaxy, and that the Milky Way is one of billions of galaxies.

The universe is so big that beams of light from the most distant regions of space take billions of years to reach us. This means we see faraway galaxies as they appeared billions of years ago, when the universe was young. The farther we look out into space, the farther we look back in time.

*Nine planets revolve
around our star, the Sun.*

**Our Solar
System**
Light-travel time
to Pluto = 6 hours

**Our Galaxy,
the Milky Way**
Light-travel time
across our galaxy =
100,000 years

### IN A GALAXY LONG AGO AND FAR AWAY
For 10 days in December 1995, astronomers aimed the Hubble Space Telescope at a tiny patch of sky near the Big Dipper (far right). The Hubble photo (near right) revealed almost 2,000 galaxies. Many of these galaxies are so far away, and the light from them takes so long to reach us, that we see them as they looked just after they formed 14 billion years ago—only a billion years after the universe itself began.

## THE VIEW BACK HOME

### LOOK CLOSELY AT EARTH...
Satellites orbiting above Earth's atmosphere can look down and see objects on Earth as small as cars. This view shows the streets, bridges, and piers of San Francisco and Oakland in California, U.S.A. The green rectangles are city parks. Dots in the harbor are ships. The shades of blue in the water show currents and silt in the harbor.

## Word Builders

The word **universe** comes from Latin words *uni-* and *versus,* meaning "one turn." The universe is everything that exists. People once thought that the Sun and the planets made up most of the universe, but by 1600 they began to understand that there were other stars like the Sun. When astronomers discovered other galaxies in the 1920s, our picture of the universe grew again.

## That's Amazing!

• If you were driving in a car at highway speeds, it would take you 340 billion years to reach the center of the Milky Way galaxy—that's more than 25 times the age of the universe.
• Earth, the Sun, and the rest of the solar system are whirling around the Milky Way galaxy at 560,000 miles per hour (900,000 km/h).

## Pathfinder

• Where does space start? Go to page 15.
• Why was Nicolaus Copernicus worried about saying Earth moved around the Sun? Go to page 22.
• What can astronomers do with variable stars? Go to page 52.
• How did the universe begin? Go to pages 60–61.

## COSMIC ZOOM

The fastest thing in the universe is a beam of light. In one second, it travels 186,000 miles (300,000 km). In one hour, it zips across 670 million miles (1,078 million km). In one year, light travels 5.9 million million miles (9.5 million million km), a distance that astronomers call one light-year. Using the speed of light as our cosmic yardstick, we can zoom to the edge of the universe in five big jumps.

*Our spiral galaxy contains about 200 billion stars.*

### INSIDE STORY

## Expanding the Universe

"You will be interested to hear that I have found a Cepheid variable in the Andromeda Nebula." With those words, Edwin Hubble announced to the world that the universe was larger than anyone had thought. The year was 1924. Hubble had found a winking variable star that allowed him to prove Andromeda is not a nebula (a cloud of dust and gas) in our galaxy, but another galaxy far away. This meant that the Milky Way is just one of many galaxies. Hubble went on to discover that the other galaxies are moving away from ours and that the universe is expanding. Today's Hubble Space Telescope is named after Edwin Hubble. Both have investigated the edge of space.

*The Local Group contains about 30 galaxies.*

**Our Galactic Cluster, the Local Group**
Light-travel time to Andromeda galaxy = 2.8 million years

**The Whole Universe**
Light-travel time to edge of universe = 15 billion years

*The universe contains as many as 50 billion galaxies.*

## THEN ZOOM AWAY...

A view from a space shuttle reveals part of the coastline of Mozambique in Africa. The red areas in this infrared image are forests and fields, and the blue and black areas are the Indian Ocean. The white streaks are plumes from forest fires that people have set deliberately to clear land for farming.

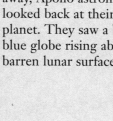

**...AND AWAY AGAIN...**
From the Moon's surface, 240,000 miles (386,000 km) away, Apollo astronauts looked back at their home planet. They saw a beautiful blue globe rising above the barren lunar surface.

**...AND EVEN FARTHER**
From 3.9 million miles (6.2 million km) away, the Galileo spacecraft showed Earth and the Moon floating in the blackness of space.

Galileo's refractor, 1609    Isaac Newton's reflector, 1671    William Herschel's big reflector, 1781

# Scoping Out Space

SPACE IS SO enormous that today's fastest rocket would take almost 100,000 years to reach the nearest star beyond the Sun. So to learn about the universe, astronomers use telescopes. Telescopes collect the light coming from distant objects and magnify it, allowing us to see the planets, stars, and galaxies as if they were much closer to us—almost as good as hopping in a starship.

The first telescopes, known as refractors, used a lens to collect light. Then in 1671, Sir Isaac Newton invented the reflecting telescope, which used a mirror to collect light. Today, most observatory telescopes are reflectors. The bigger the mirror, the more light it can collect, so bigger telescopes can show us objects that are fainter and farther away. Many observatories are now building monster scopes that will use mirrors as wide as houses.

Not all telescopes collect the kind of light that our eyes can see. Planets, stars, and galaxies also send out invisible waves, such as radio beams and X-rays. In the past 50 years, astronomers have invented telescopes that can detect this invisible radiation. The air above us blocks some of the waves, so astronomers place infrared, ultraviolet, and X-ray telescopes in orbit high above our atmosphere. These space telescopes have revealed strange objects, such as exploding galaxies and black holes, that no one knew existed.

HANDS ON

## Looking Up

You don't need the Hubble Space Telescope to explore space. With nothing but your eyes, you can gaze at the stars and find ancient constellations, such as Orion the Hunter, or Leo the Lion. You can also see five of the planets, watch the Moon go from crescent to full, or spot a streaking meteor.

Binoculars show as much detail as Galileo saw through his simple telescope. They let you follow the moons of Jupiter, admire the many stars of the Milky Way, or find the fuzzy Orion Nebula.

A telescope reveals even more—from Saturn's rings and Jupiter's clouds to the spiral arms of the Andromeda galaxy. If you want to look through a telescope or just ask questions about the night sky, contact your local observatory, planetarium, or science center.

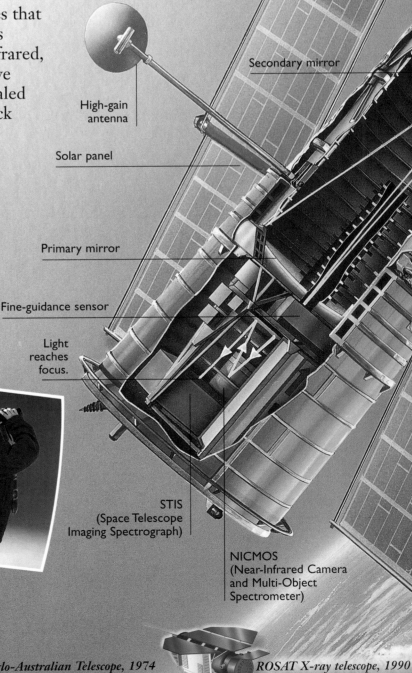

High-gain antenna

Solar panel

Secondary mirror

Primary mirror

Fine-guidance sensor

Light reaches focus.

STIS (Space Telescope Imaging Spectrograph)

NICMOS (Near-Infrared Camera and Multi-Object Spectrometer)

Green Bank radio telescope, 1965    Anglo-Australian Telescope, 1974    ROSAT X-ray telescope, 1990

## Word Builders

Galileo was the first person ever to use a telescope for astronomy, but he called his instrument a spyglass. In 1611, at a banquet that was held in Galileo's honor, a Greek poet named John Demisiani suggested the name **telescope,** from two Greek words, *tele* and *skopein,* meaning "to view far off."

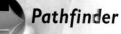

## That's Amazing!

• With four 27-foot (8.2-m) mirrors, the Very Large Telescope, when it is first used in 2001, will become the largest optical telescope on Earth.
• When launched into orbit past the Moon after 2007, the Next Generation Space Telescope may use a mirror 26 feet (8 m) across that will unfold like the petals of a flower.

## Pathfinder

• What amazing photos has the Hubble Space Telescope taken? Go to pages 8, 52–53, and 54–55.
• Are radio telescopes listening for extraterrestrial broadcasts? Go to page 19.
• For more skywatching tips, go to pages 30, 37, 44, 48–49, 55, and 57.

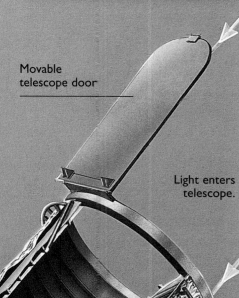

Movable telescope door

Light enters telescope.

### EAGLE EYE IN THE SKY

Our atmosphere blurs the view seen through telescopes on the ground, so astronomers placed the Hubble Space Telescope above the atmosphere. Hubble is about as big as a school bus, orbits Earth every 90 minutes, and provides the sharpest pictures of stars and galaxies ever taken. It uses electronic cameras with tongue-twisting names like Near-Infrared Camera and Multi-Object Spectrometer to take digital pictures. The telescope then transmits the pictures by radio to mission control on Earth. Every three years, astronauts visit Hubble in a space shuttle to repair or replace old parts.

### SEEING THE INVISIBLE

Like a single note on a piano, light is just one type of radiation coming from space. Objects in the universe send out an entire keyboard of radiation. If our eyes could detect these invisible waves, we would see a very different universe.

### THE RADIO UNIVERSE

We use radio waves to broadcast music and TV. Objects in space with strong magnetism also send out radio waves. In this radio picture of Jupiter, we see the planet's giant magnetic field.

High-gain antenna

### WIDE EYES ON THE MOUNTAINS

Astronomers build telescopes where the sky is clear—on mountaintops far from city lights. The summit of Mauna Kea in Hawaii, U.S.A., is home to many optical telescopes (the kind that collect visible light). Each of the two Keck Telescopes uses a mirror 33 feet (10 m) across, making them the biggest optical telescopes in the world. They are housed in two large domes.

### THE INFRARED UNIVERSE

Warm objects, like just-popped toast, send out infrared radiation, or heat. Infrared pictures, such as this one of Saturn, tell us the temperature of objects and allow us to peer through thick clouds of dust in space.

### BIG EARS ON THE COSMOS

The Very Large Array (VLA) in New Mexico, U.S.A., is one of the world's largest radio telescopes. Its 27 dish-shaped antennas can tune in to crackling radio signals coming from planets, stars, and galaxies. Astronomers have used radio telescopes like the VLA to map the shape of our Milky Way galaxy.

### THE X-RAY UNIVERSE

Doctors and dentists use X-rays to examine our bodies and teeth. Astronomers use X-ray telescopes to watch superhot gas falling into black holes, as in the star Cygnus X-1, shown in this X-ray photo.

*Vostok, 1961*　　　*Gemini, 1965*　　　*Soyuz, 1967*　　　*Future space plane*

# Blast Off!

WHILE TELESCOPES LET astronomers look at distant galaxies, rockets allow people to explore nearby space. The first person to travel into space was the Soviet Union's Yuri Gagarin, in 1961. The United States and the Soviet Union then raced to put a human on the Moon. The space race ended in 1969, when an American, Neil Armstrong, stepped onto the lunar surface.

To soar high enough to start orbiting Earth, a spacecraft needs speed. If it goes any slower than 17,000 miles per hour (28,000 km/h), the spacecraft will fall back to the ground. Only rocket-powered spacecraft travel fast enough to reach space. Most are made of several stages that drop off, leaving a light upper stage to reach orbit. In the future, rocket-powered space planes will reach orbit with just a single stage.

The National Aeronautics and Space Administration (NASA) now has four space shuttles. The shuttles can orbit Earth but they cannot travel any farther. The Saturn V rocket propelled people to the Moon on Apollo missions, but the last Saturn V was launched in 1973. Future rockets will allow people to travel back to the Moon and past it to Mars.

## A FAR-OUT GOLF COURSE

From 1968 to 1972, 27 astronauts visited the Moon in the Apollo spacecraft. During most missions, two astronauts landed using the lunar module while one astronaut orbited overhead in the command module. In 1971, during the Apollo 14 mission, Alan Shepard played golf on the Moon. He made a golf club from a rock-collecting tool and hit a ball "miles and miles."

## HANDS ON
### Launch a Rocket

It's easy to show how a rocket launch works.

❶ Blow up a party balloon and squeeze the neck of the balloon between your fingers so the air can't get out.

❷ Point the balloon toward the ceiling and let go. As the air escapes, it pushes the balloon forward.

Instead of air, a rocket uses hot gases for propulsion. Its engines burn fuel to make the gases, which spew out the exhaust. These gases push against the rocket and force it to lift off.

## SPLASHDOWN!

During the American space missions of the 1960s and 1970s, astronauts returned to Earth in capsules that splashed down into the ocean. The astronauts then had to be fished out by helicopters. Today's shuttles land at runways, as will future space planes. Astronauts walk off like passengers disembarking from a jet airliner.

## FLYING THE SPACE SHUTTLE

### LIFTOFF
You are about to blast off on the shuttle. Hold on! At Takeoff Time (T) minus 6.6 seconds, the three main engines fire. At T equals 0, the two solid rocket boosters (SRBs) ignite, and the space shuttle takes off.

### SRB SEPARATION
With a bang at T plus 2 minutes, the SRBs burn out and shoot away from the shuttle. They parachute back to Earth, where they will be collected. The ride becomes smooth and quiet.

### TANK FALLS AWAY
The main engines are powered by liquid hydrogen and oxygen from the external tank. At T plus 8.5 minutes, the engines shut off. Its fuel gone, the external tank falls into the Pacific Ocean.

## Word Builders

People who fly on American space missions are called **astronauts,** from two Greek words, *astron* and *nautes,* meaning "star voyagers." Russians, and others from the former Soviet Union, who fly into space are called **cosmonauts,** meaning "voyagers into the cosmos." Now the two kinds of voyagers fly together on joint missions.

## That's Amazing!

• The last two Saturn Vs, the only rockets able to send people to the Moon, are now museum displays at NASA in Houston and Cape Canaveral.
• During launch, a space shuttle burns up to 10 tons of fuel every second.
• Nearly 28,000 ceramic tiles protect the shuttle from the intense heat of reentry.

## Pathfinder

• What does it feel like to be in zero gravity? Go to page 15.
• What other machines can explore space? Go to pages 16–17.
• What was it like to walk on the Moon? Go to page 26.
• Will people ever travel to Mars? Go to page 32.

**DOGS IN SPACE**
Belka and Strelka, two Russian dogs, were the first creatures to return to Earth after orbiting it. They flew aboard Korabl-Sputnik 2 in August 1960, eight months before cosmonaut Yuri Gagarin boarded the Vostok 1 spacecraft and became the first person in space.

### INSIDE STORY
## Wild Ride into Space

"A shuttle launch is unlike anything I've ever experienced on Earth," explains commander Eileen Collins. "You *see* smoke around the shuttle on liftoff, then bright flashes of light, like a lightning storm, for the next eight and a half minutes. You *hear* fire. You *smell* electrical components and dry air. You *feel* your back aching after spending four hours lying vertical during countdown. Then, during the ascent, you are hurled into space faster and faster. Breathing is difficult. Reaching and moving is difficult. But suddenly the acceleration cuts off, and you are in zero gravity."

**IN ORBIT**
Once in orbit, the payload-bay doors open, and you're ready to begin work. Traveling at about 17,500 miles per hour (28,000 km/h), the shuttle orbits Earth every 90 minutes.

**REENTRY**
Time to come home. As you descend at 25 times the speed of sound, the shuttle surface and the air around it glow red hot. The thickening atmosphere slows the shuttle to aircraft speed.

**TOUCHDOWN**
The shuttle uses its wings to glide down through the atmosphere. Just above the landing strip, the shuttle's wheels extend. Moments later, you touch down. Welcome home!

13

# Working in Space

SHUTTLE ASTRONAUTS HAVE only a little time to enjoy the view of Earth below while they're in space. There's always work to do! They conduct long, complicated experiments, testing how zero gravity affects people or how to make new materials such as ultrapure crystals or medicines. On some missions, astronauts release satellites for observing Earth, the Sun, or the stars. Space work can also involve an extravehicular activity (EVA)—in other words, a spacewalk—to repair satellites or assemble space station parts.

Flights on a space shuttle last only a week or two, but cosmonauts and astronauts can spend months on a space station. Here they conduct much longer experiments. Life on a space station can be draining—the lack of gravity affects the flow of blood, wastes away muscles, and weakens bones. Space station residents must exercise for hours every day to keep their bodies strong.

Along with space shuttles and space stations, hundreds of satellites are working in space. Some were put into orbit by space shuttles, but most were lofted into space by rockets. Satellites make it possible to send TV pictures around the world instantly, to navigate ships across the ocean, or to predict the weather days in advance. We now depend on these eyes and ears in the sky.

### FLYING FOOD
Some food on the shuttle is ready to eat, and some is like dehydrated camping food—you just need to add water. A typical day's menu includes a breakfast of orange drink, scrambled eggs, and a sweet roll; a lunch of soup, sandwich, banana, and cookies; and a dinner of beefsteak, broccoli, pudding, and cocoa. Here Michael Baker grabs a bite of lunch—a free-floating peanut butter and jelly sandwich.

### DRESSED FOR SPACE
A spacesuit is like a miniature spaceship. Tanks in the backpack supply oxygen for breathing. Layers of Kevlar, Teflon, and Dacron insulate the astronaut from the extreme temperatures— 250°F (120°C) in sunlight and –250°F (–156°C) in shadow. The suit blocks the Sun's radiation and keeps out tiny bits of space dust. Water pumped through tubes in the underwear keeps the hard-working astronaut cool. The astronaut can sip water from a drink container, munch on a snack bar, and talk to the other astronauts through a headset called a Snoopy cap. On Earth, the entire suit weighs more than an astronaut, but in orbit, it weighs nothing.

Spandex mesh underwear

Water-cooling tubes

Spacesuit made of several layers

Urine collection device

Tool kit

Visor and helmet

Primary life-support-system backpack

Cordless electric screwdriver

Lights on helmet

## Word Builders

Astronauts feel weightless because they are always in **free fall** around Earth. Anything falling from a great height feels weightless—for a few seconds—until it hits the ground! But objects in orbit are so high and traveling so fast that they never hit Earth. They experience **zero G,** or zero gravity, more correctly called **microgravity.**

## That's Amazing!

• During weightlessness, the vertebrae of the spine spread apart. Astronauts grow 1–2 inches (2.5–5 cm) taller during a space flight. When they return to Earth, astronauts shrink back to preflight size.
• Space toilets can't use water to flush, so they use air. They are like vacuum cleaners that you sit on.

## Pathfinder

• Why do astronauts visit the Hubble Space Telescope? Go to page 11.
• How do astronauts get into space? Go to pages 12–13.
• What would it be like to be the first astronaut on Mars? Go to page 32.
• How can an astronomy satellite help to explain how the universe formed? Go to page 60.

### LABORATORY IN THE SKY
The International Space Station will replace the Russian Mir space station. This new station will be gradually assembled in space during 45 visits from United States space shuttles and Russian Proton rockets. When completed in 2004, the station will be as big as a football field and home to astronauts and scientists from around the world.

Display and control module

Metal airtight collars

Gloves

Snoopy cap for communication

### SPACE WORK NEVER ENDS
On the space shuttle's Microgravity Laboratory in 1995, Catherine Coleman and six other astronauts tested the effects of zero gravity on many different materials. Astronaut John Glenn tested the effects of zero gravity on older people during a 1998 shuttle mission.

Last traces of atmosphere 600 miles (1,000 km)

Hubble Space Telescope 370 miles (600 km)

Space shuttle 120–370 miles (200–600 km)

International Space Station 220 miles (350 km)

Aurora 90–300 miles (150–500 km)

Low Earth-orbiting satellite 85 miles (300 km)

Meteor shower 50 miles (80 km)

Concorde 9 miles (15 km)

Clouds 4–6 miles (6–10 km)

Jumbo jet 6 miles (10 km)

Mount Everest 5.5 miles (8.8 km)

## INSIDE STORY

# A Day in Space

In 1998, Australian-born Andrew Thomas spent five months on Mir, the Russian space station. "Although we see the Sun rise sixteen times a day," explained Thomas, "we get up at 8:30 AM Moscow Time. To wash, we can't splash water because it would float everywhere. So we use a damp washcloth. After breakfast we work on our experiments. By 7:00 PM it's time for dinner. Then I watch the world go by out the window. We are in bed by 11:00 PM, in bags we tie to a wall."

## WHERE DOES SPACE START?
No sharp line divides air and space. The atmosphere just gets thinner as you go up. On Mount Everest, the air is so thin that climbers use bottled oxygen. But even 200 miles (320 km) up, there are still a few oxygen and nitrogen molecules. The drag from these molecules would make a space station fall to Earth, so the station needs a boost from its rockets every few months. Above 600 miles (1,000 km), satellites circle beyond the last bits of air and can orbit for many years.

# Robot Probes

MOST PLANETS, COMETS, and asteroids are too far away to visit in person, but we still want to learn more about them. Because it would be too dangerous and expensive to send astronauts, we send remote-controlled robot probes instead.

Most of our knowledge about the planets has come from these robots, which first visited Venus and Mars in the 1960s. Some probes orbit a planet—Magellan orbited Venus. A few, such as the Galileo Probe at Jupiter, enter the planet's atmosphere, while probes like Mars Pathfinder actually land on the planet. Others fly past the planet—Voyager studied Jupiter, Saturn, Uranus, and Neptune on a flyby. While probes are zooming past a planet, they get a boost in speed from its gravity and can then fly on toward a more distant planet. Using this slingshot method, we have now sent probes to every planet in the solar system except tiny Pluto.

Robot probes can also explore other objects in the solar system. Future probes are expected to land on comets, hop across an asteroid, and zoom through the hot atmosphere of the Sun. So far, no robot probe has returned to Earth. Instead, probes send their digital pictures and data to Earth as radio waves, and the signals are picked up by giant radio telescopes. In the future, though, some probes will carry samples from Mars, comets, and asteroids back to Earth.

## HANDS ON
### Probe the Web

The best way to keep up to date on planet missions is to explore the World Wide Web, where you can find the very latest information, along with loads of pictures of robot probes and the planets they have visited. A good place to start is the web site of NASA's Jet Propulsion Laboratory—*www.jpl.nasa.gov.* From here, links take you to prior missions such as Magellan (Venus) and Mars Pathfinder; current missions such as Cassini (Saturn) and Galileo (Jupiter); and future missions such as Pluto-Kuiper Express and Stardust (comets). When the Sojourner rover visited Mars in 1997, its pictures were immediately displayed on the Web. The busiest day saw the NASA web site deluged with 47 million hits—more than any other web site has ever received.

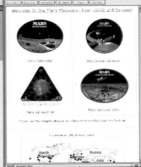

### ROVING AROUND MARS

In July 1997, the first rover to visit another planet rolled off the Pathfinder lander and onto the surface of Mars. Called Sojourner, the rover used cameras and a cuplike detector to look at rocks up close and found evidence that water had gushed across Mars billions of years ago. Sojourner's mission ended three months later when the Pathfinder lander, which commanded the rover, became too cold and stopped working.

# Word Builders

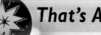

Space probes are named in a variety of ways. **Galileo, Cassini,** and **Huygens** are named for astronomers. Some probe names, such as **Ulysses,** come from mythology. **Magellan** is named for an explorer; **Giotto** for a painter who depicted Comet Halley. The **Clementine** probe was named for a song character in "Darling Clementine."

# That's Amazing!

• Pioneer 10, the first probe to reach Jupiter, is now heading for the star Aldebaran, which is 65 light-years from Earth. The probe will take more than two million years to reach the star.
• The billion-dollar Mars Observer probe blew up just as it approached Mars in 1993. It had taken only one picture.

# Pathfinder

• How did Magellan see through the clouds of Venus? Go to pages 30–31.
• What is a nanorover and where is it going? Go to pages 34–35
• What messages are the two Voyager probes carrying? Go to page 41.
• When will a probe visit Pluto? Go to pages 42–43.
• How will a probe collect comet dust? Go to pages 44–45.

## MAPPING MARS

Just as the Mars Pathfinder lander mission was ending in 1997, Global Surveyor arrived to orbit Mars. Its four-year mission is to map the entire planet with cameras that can see objects on Mars as small as a house.

## BUILDING A PROBE

Hundreds of people work together to build a space probe. Once it is flying toward its target, the robot probe is beyond the reach of astronauts, so all its parts must work for many years without repair. The European Ulysses probe, shown here, was launched in 1990 and should keep exploring the polar regions of the Sun until 2001.

# GETTING DOWN TO TITAN

Cassini, a spacecraft the size of a truck, began its trip to Saturn in 1997. It is scheduled to arrive on July 1, 2004. Attached to Cassini's side is a probe called Huygens. Here's what Huygens will do.

## PROBE AWAY

On November 6, 2004, Cassini releases the Huygens probe. Its destination is Titan, Saturn's largest moon.

| Cassini | Huygens |

## HOT FLIGHT

Three weeks later, Huygens plows into Titan's thick atmosphere at 12,000 miles per hour (20,000 km/h). Huygens's heat shield becomes twice as hot as the Sun.

Heat shield

## PUTTING ON THE BRAKES

With Huygens slowed to 900 miles per hour (1,400 km/h), a small parachute opens.

## MAIN CHUTE POPS

A large parachute further slows Huygens. Fifteen minutes later, it is discarded.

Heat shield is released.

## BELOW THE CLOUDS

The last descent on a small chute takes two hours. Huygens's cameras snap pictures of the surface below.

## TOUCHDOWN!

Huygens lands on ice or splashes into a lake of liquid methane. It sends back a few pictures, but survives no more than 30 minutes.

## INSIDE STORY

## Explorer of the Planets

"In our time we've crossed the Solar System," wrote Carl Sagan. Best known for explaining space to millions of people through his books and TV shows, Carl Sagan also helped plan many missions to the planets. He eloquently described the significance of robot probes: "These spacecraft have taught us about the wonders of other worlds, about the uniqueness and fragility of our own, about beginnings and ends. They have given us access to most of the Solar System.... They are the ships that first explored what may be the homelands of our remote descendants." After Carl Sagan died in 1996, NASA honored him by giving the Mars Pathfinder lander a new name—it is now called the Sagan Memorial Station.

# Looking for Life

WHEN YOU GAZE at the stars, you might find yourself asking the big question—are we alone? We find life everywhere on Earth, even in unlikely places such as deep oil wells, pools of boiling water, and inside Antarctic rocks. Has life also adapted to the extreme conditions on other planets? It seems possible, but where do we look?

All life that we know requires water. Mars had oceans of water billions of years ago. Perhaps life started there but died out. One of Jupiter's moons, Europa, might have an ocean under its icy crust. And Titan, a smoggy moon of Saturn, is rich in the carbon compounds that started life on Earth. It may also be made partly of water ice.

In recent years, astronomers have found dozens of planets orbiting other stars. These planets are not places like Earth. They are all giant worlds, like Jupiter, where life is unlikely to exist. But perhaps astronomers will find Earth-like planets, too. Future space telescopes will be able to take pictures of these smaller planets, if they exist.

Some astronomers suggest that our galaxy could contain as many as one million other civilizations. Are aliens visiting Earth now in UFOs? Most scientists think that UFOs can be explained in other ways. But perhaps in your lifetime, we will find proof that aliens exist.

## INSIDE STORY
### Seeing Signs of Martians

One hundred years ago, Percival Lowell was sure that Martians were real. "The telescope presents us with perhaps the most startling discovery of modern times—the canals of Mars," he wrote. Lowell saw lines crisscrossing Mars. He thought they must be canals built by intelligent beings. "What we see hints at the existence of beings who are in advance of, not behind us, in the journey of life." But the canals were not real—they were optical illusions. Although Lowell was wrong, his ideas sparked interest in Mars that continues to this day.

### ALIEN IDEAS
Here are some guesses of what aliens might look like. Of course, they could be unlike any life we know, or might not exist at all.

### SMART REPTILES
Perhaps advanced dinosaurs would dominate on Earth-like planets. Some scientists think that if Earth's dinosaurs had not become extinct, they might have evolved into intelligent, upright creatures.

### GAS GIANT FLOATERS
On gas giant planets, perhaps there would be creatures that float in the dense atmosphere, like fish that swim in our seas.

## Word Builders

Space exploration uses many acronyms—short words that stand for a longer phrase.
• The acronym **SETI** (which is pronounced *set-tee*) stands for "Search for Extra Terrestrial Intelligence."
• Extra Terrestrial, as in **ET,** means "from beyond Earth."
• The acronym **UFO** stands for "Unidentified Flying Object."

## That's Amazing!

• In 1974, astronomers used the Arecibo radio telescope to beam a message to M13, a star cluster so far away that if aliens get our message and respond, we won't receive their reply until the year AD 44,000.
• As late as 1965, people thought that some kind of canals might exist on Mars. It took the first Mars probe, Mariner 4, to prove that water-filled Martian canals don't exist.

## Pathfinder

• What else do we use radio telescopes for? Go to pages 10–11.
• When will we investigate Titan? Go to page 17.
• How did a Martian meteorite get to Earth? Go to page 33.
• Which probes have investigated Jupiter's moon Europa? Go to page 37.
• Who discovered planets around other stars? Go to page 51.

### LISTENING FOR LIFE

Scientists with Project Phoenix and other SETI programs use radio telescopes around the world to search for signals from alien civilizations. If such a signal was detected, it would be the greatest discovery of all time—but would we be able to decode it?

### BUGS ON MARS?

Is this a Martian life form? In 1996, a team of scientists announced that they had discovered fossilized bacteria in a meteorite from Mars. Other scientists doubt the results and think that the evidence has other explanations. The debate may continue until we get more rocks from Mars to study.

### HANDS ON
## Recipe for a Titanite

Create an alien that might live on Titan, one of Saturn's moons. You can use modeling clay or common household items such as old boxes, foil, and straws. Think about what the Titanite eats, how it moves around, how it avoids predators, how it copes with the temperature, and how it breathes, sees, and hears. Keep in mind what Titan is like as you create your Titanite.
• Titan is extremely cold—about −289°F (−178°C).
• Titan is covered in thick smog, and the nitrogen atmosphere does not contain any oxygen.
• The surface is probably rocky, icy, and cratered.
• Almost all water on Titan is frozen, but there may be seas of sticky red-brown liquid methane, as well as methane clouds, rain, and snow.

### UNDER THE ICE OF EUROPA

A crust of cracked ice covers Europa, one of Jupiter's moons. Underneath the ice, there may be an ocean of liquid water, heated from below by volcanic vents. In Earth's deepest oceans, strange worms, blind fish, and heat-loving bacteria thrive in the darkness around volcanic vents. Could Europa harbor life in its dark ocean? A submarinelike probe now being planned could find out.

### LOW-G LIFE

On low-density planets with weak gravity, life forms might resemble giraffes, with tall, spindly bodies. Like us, intelligent aliens would probably have two arms and two legs, because it is a simple but efficient body design.

### HIGH-G ALIENS

The gravity on large, dense planets is strong. Aliens there might be squat, slow-moving creatures, with elephantlike legs and a strong tail to support their weight.

# Our Solar
# System

You are about to travel through your cosmic neighborhood. Here you will find Earth's neighbors—the other planets, their moons, and the asteroids and comets—all circling our nearest star, the Sun. Your tour begins with something very familiar—our own planet Earth and the Moon. You then shoot to the center of our solar system with a visit to the scorching Sun. Hold on tight. The journey continues to the nearby rocky planets, the asteroid belt, and the distant gas giant planets. Your tour ends with Pluto and the comets at the cold, dark edges of the solar system.

page **22** How big is the Sun compared to these planets?

Go to THE SUN'S FAMILY.

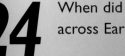

page **24** When did this dinosaur walk across Earth?

Go to OUR PLANET EARTH.

page **26** This huge collision happened more than four billion years ago. What happened next?

Go to OUR MOON.

page **28** Which part of the Sun can you see in this photo?

Go to THE SUN.

page **30** How did scientists make a map of cloud-covered Venus?

Go to MERCURY AND VENUS.

*page* **32**

People once thought these aliens were invading a planet. Which planet?

Go to **MARS**.

*page* **34**

How can an asteroid darken the skies of Earth?

Go to **ASTEROIDS AND METEOROIDS**.

*page* **36**

What smashed into the planet Jupiter in 1994?

Go to **JUPITER**.

*page* **38**

Why are there so many small rocks near this planet? What happened to them?

Go to **SATURN**.

*page* **40**

What are the messages on this disc? Who might read them?

Go to **URANUS AND NEPTUNE**.

*page* **42**

How big is the spacecraft that will visit Pluto and its moon, Charon?

Go to **PLUTO AND BEYOND**.

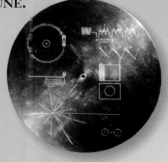

*page* **44**

This comet displays two tails—a blue one and a yellowish one. What are the tails made of?

Go to **COMETS**.

# The Sun's Family

YOU BELONG TO a cosmic family called the solar system. The Sun heads this collection of nine planets, dozens of moons, and countless asteroids and comets. The biggest and best-known family members are the planets, and the planet we know best is Earth itself. You can see five of the planets with the naked eye because they shine brightly in our sky. These are Mercury, Venus, Mars, Jupiter, and Saturn. The other three—Uranus, Neptune, and Pluto—lie so far from the Sun that you need binoculars, or even a telescope, to see them.

Most planets aren't alone in space. Seven of the planets have companions called moons. Earth has one moon. Saturn has the most—18 in total. Only Mercury and Venus travel around the Sun without any moons.

Many other worlds belong to the Sun's family. Thousands of rocky minor planets called asteroids move in a belt between Mars and Jupiter. Some small asteroids travel close to the Sun. At the edge of the solar system, past Pluto, there are millions of ice balls. When one of these shoots toward the Sun, we may see it as a comet with a glowing tail of gas and dust.

## INSIDE STORY

## The Man Who Moved Earth

The year is 1543. Everyone believes Earth is the center of the solar system, but you have a different theory. "It is in the very center of all the planets," you write, "that the Sun finds its place." You suggest that Earth and the other planets move around the Sun. Your theory shifts Earth from the center of the universe. You know people won't like your ideas. They might even arrest you. What do you do? Astronomer Nicolaus Copernicus faced that question more than 450 years ago. To avoid trouble, he waited until he was dying to publish his theory. Nearly 100 years passed before people accepted his ideas.

NICOLAS COPERNIC

### GOING AROUND AND AROUND

Gravity, a powerful pull from the Sun, holds the planets, comets, and asteroids in paths called orbits. These orbits are ellipses, like squashed circles. As planets orbit the Sun, they spin like tops. One trip around the Sun is a planet's year. A planet's day is the time it takes to spin around once. Earth's year is about 365 days. Pluto pokes along, taking 248 Earth years to complete its year, but Sun-hugging Mercury whips around the Sun in 88 days.

**Pluto**
Distance from Sun:
3,676 million miles
(5,916 million km)
One day: 6.4 Earth days
One year: 248 Earth years

**Neptune**
Distance from Sun:
2,799 million miles
(4,504 million km)
One day: 16.1 Earth hours
One year: 163.7 Earth years

**Uranus**
Distance from Sun:
1,787 million miles
(2,875 million km)
One day: 17.2 Earth hours
One year: 83.8 Earth years

## HANDS ON

## Pacing Out the Solar System

You can make your own model of the solar system with a peppercorn, two peas, two small marbles, two limes, an orange, a grapefruit, and a blow-up beachball.

Put the beachball on a long pavement. The ball stands for the Sun. Take one step and put down a pea for Mercury. Take another step and put down a marble for Venus, then a half step and another marble for Earth, our home.

Just one and one-half steps on from Earth, put down a pea for Mars. Then take nine steps before plunking down the grapefruit for Jupiter. Eleven steps after Jupiter, place the orange for Saturn. After 24 more steps, add a lime for Uranus, and 27 steps later, put down the other lime for Neptune. Finally, add a peppercorn for tiny Pluto, 24 steps after Neptune—and 99 steps from the beachball Sun.

The solar system is big! If Pluto were really just 99 steps from the Sun, the Sun would be no bigger than a marble and all the planets would be tiny specks.

### PLANETS BIG AND SMALL

There are two kinds of planets. Giant Jupiter, Saturn, Uranus, and Neptune are balls of gas far from the Sun. Mercury, Venus, Mars, and our own planet, Earth, are small rocky planets close to the Sun. Pluto, the smallest planet, doesn't fit in. It's a tiny ice world at the edge of the solar system. The size comparison at right lists each planet's diameter (the distance across the planet). You can see that even Jupiter, the biggest planet, is small next to the Sun.

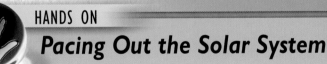

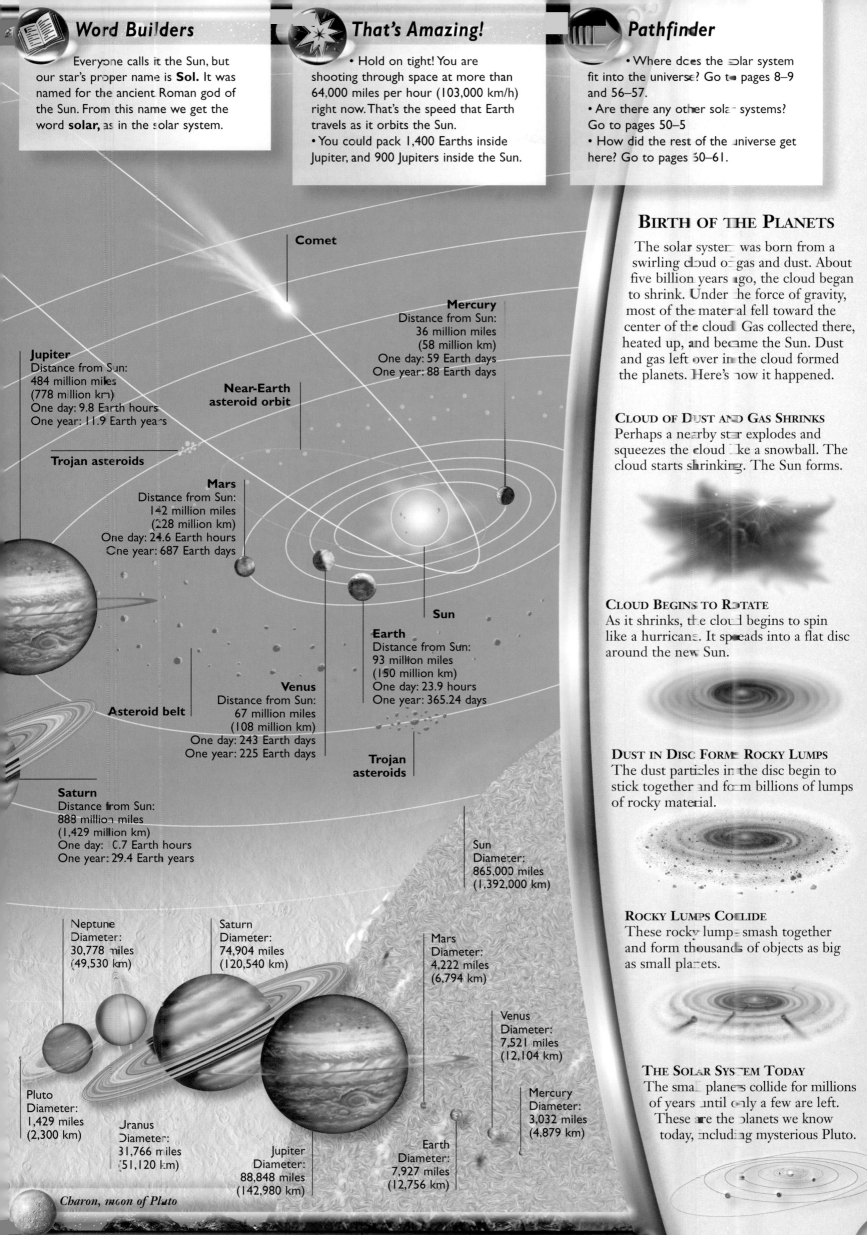

## Word Builders

Everyone calls it the Sun, but our star's proper name is **Sol.** It was named for the ancient Roman god of the Sun. From this name we get the word **solar,** as in the solar system.

## That's Amazing!

• Hold on tight! You are shooting through space at more than 64,000 miles per hour (103,000 km/h) right now. That's the speed that Earth travels as it orbits the Sun.
• You could pack 1,400 Earths inside Jupiter, and 900 Jupiters inside the Sun.

## Pathfinder

• Where does the solar system fit into the universe? Go to pages 8–9 and 56–57.
• Are there any other solar systems? Go to pages 50–5
• How did the rest of the universe get here? Go to pages 60–61.

**Comet**

**Jupiter**
Distance from Sun:
484 million miles
(778 million km)
One day: 9.8 Earth hours
One year: 11.9 Earth years

**Trojan asteroids**

**Near-Earth asteroid orbit**

**Mercury**
Distance from Sun:
36 million miles
(58 million km)
One day: 59 Earth days
One year: 88 Earth days

**Mars**
Distance from Sun:
142 million miles
(228 million km)
One day: 24.6 Earth hours
One year: 687 Earth days

**Sun**

**Earth**
Distance from Sun:
93 million miles
(150 million km)
One day: 23.9 hours
One year: 365.24 days

**Venus**
Distance from Sun:
67 million miles
(108 million km)
One day: 243 Earth days
One year: 225 Earth days

**Asteroid belt**

**Trojan asteroids**

**Saturn**
Distance from Sun:
888 million miles
(1,429 million km)
One day: 10.7 Earth hours
One year: 29.4 Earth years

**Sun**
Diameter:
865,000 miles
(1,392,000 km)

**Neptune**
Diameter:
30,778 miles
(49,530 km)

**Saturn**
Diameter:
74,904 miles
(120,540 km)

**Mars**
Diameter:
4,222 miles
(6,794 km)

**Venus**
Diameter:
7,521 miles
(12,104 km)

**Pluto**
Diameter:
1,429 miles
(2,300 km)

**Uranus**
Diameter:
31,766 miles
(51,120 km)

**Jupiter**
Diameter:
88,848 miles
(142,980 km)

**Earth**
Diameter:
7,927 miles
(12,756 km)

**Mercury**
Diameter:
3,032 miles
(4,879 km)

*Charon, moon of Pluto*

## BIRTH OF THE PLANETS

The solar system was born from a swirling cloud of gas and dust. About five billion years ago, the cloud began to shrink. Under the force of gravity, most of the material fell toward the center of the cloud. Gas collected there, heated up, and became the Sun. Dust and gas left over in the cloud formed the planets. Here's how it happened.

### CLOUD OF DUST AND GAS SHRINKS
Perhaps a nearby star explodes and squeezes the cloud like a snowball. The cloud starts shrinking. The Sun forms.

### CLOUD BEGINS TO ROTATE
As it shrinks, the cloud begins to spin like a hurricane. It spreads into a flat disc around the new Sun.

### DUST IN DISC FORMS ROCKY LUMPS
The dust particles in the disc begin to stick together and form billions of lumps of rocky material.

### ROCKY LUMPS COLLIDE
These rocky lumps smash together and form thousands of objects as big as small planets.

### THE SOLAR SYSTEM TODAY
The small planets collide for millions of years until only a few are left. These are the planets we know today, including mysterious Pluto.

# Our Planet Earth

HAVE YOU EVER thought of Earth as speeding through space? We live on the third planet from the Sun. Like the other planets, Earth orbits the Sun. It also spins on its axis. But Earth is unique because it is the only planet with the right conditions for life.

Planets closer to the Sun are too hot for living things. Those farther from the Sun are too cold. Some planets have an atmosphere too poisonous to breathe—or no atmosphere at all. And some, like Jupiter and Saturn, have no solid surface to walk on. But here on Earth, you can breathe the air, see a blue sky, splash in a pool of water, or pick an apple from a tree. Earth is the only planet where you can do these things.

The world you see around you is constantly changing. Earth is a rocky planet like Mercury, Venus, and Mars, but it is much more active. Heat from deep inside our planet forces volcanoes to erupt, earthquakes to shake the surface, and the continents to shift slowly over time. Meanwhile, wind, rain, and ocean waves gradually reshape the landscape.

### THE BIG MARBLE

In this view from the cargo bay of the space shuttle, the shuttle's tail points back toward our planet, which looks like a big, beautiful marble floating in space. The blue is the oceans, with their rippling waves and sea currents. The white is the clouds—puffy fair-weather clouds as well as raging hurricanes. The rich reds, browns, and greens are the deserts, plains, forests, and cities of our planet.

### INSIDE EARTH

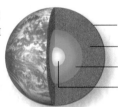

— Rocky crust
— Rocky mantle
— Liquid iron/nickel outer core
— Solid iron/nickel inner core

## HANDS ON

### Following Shadows

As Earth spins, the Sun appears to move across the sky and the shadows you see change. By following the shadows, you can tell that Earth is spinning and can even tell the time of day.

❶ On a sunny day, push a wooden pole into the ground.

❷ Every hour, use a Popsicle stick to mark where the pole's shadow falls. Write the hour on the stick.

❸ Position several Popsicle sticks to make a sunclock.

Check the shadow of the pole over the next week or so and it will tell you the time.

## A SHORT HISTORY OF EARTH

### 4.6 TO 4 BILLION YEARS AGO

Asteroids and comets rain down on the young Earth. The heat from their impacts keeps the surface red-hot and flowing with molten lava. Gases from volcanoes make a choking atmosphere. Primitive oceans form, only to boil off as vapor. Life is impossible.

Asteroids pelt the young Earth.

### 3.8 BILLION YEARS AGO

The big impacts from asteroids and comets end. Earth cools off, and oceans form. The water comes from the debris of icy comets and from volcanic gases that condense into rain. Chemicals combine in the oceans to form single cells, the first life on Earth. Later, simple plants fill the air with oxygen.

Life begins in early oceans.

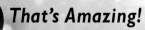

## Word Builders

No single person named our planet. Many ancient people called the world after their god or goddess of the soil or fertility. The name **Earth** comes from the Anglo-Saxon word *eorthe*, meaning "land." But liquid water covers nearly three-quarters of the globe, so perhaps we should call our planet Ocean!

## That's Amazing!

• The faster a planet turns, the shorter its day is. Three billion years ago, Earth turned much faster, and its day was only 18 hours long.
• Wind and rain have worn away most of Earth's impact craters. If Earth had no atmosphere to create weather, it would have as many craters as the Moon.

## Pathfinder

• How would it feel to take off in the space shuttle? Go to pages 12–13.
• Is there any other life in the universe? Go to pages 18–19.
• Was the Moon once part of Earth? Go to page 27.
• Which other planet is the most like Earth? Go to pages 32–33

### NIGHT AND DAY

The spinning, or rotation, of Earth every 24 hours brings us night and day. To see how Earth's rotation works, spin around on a sunny day. First your face is lit up by the Sun. Then your face moves into shadow. The same thing happens to Earth. The part of Earth where you live faces the Sun during the daytime. As your place on Earth turns away from the Sun, it becomes night.

### INSIDE STORY

## The View from Space

The best part of traveling into space is the view back home. "It's hard to explain how magical this experience is," said astronaut Kathy Sullivan after her 1990 shuttle mission. "If you float up by the forward seats, you have six large windows providing a spectacular panorama of the Earth below. On my second shuttle flight, we could see all the way up to the Great Lakes from over the Gulf of Mexico. You can see rivers, cities, even airports. At night, you can even use the lights of highways and cities to locate your hometown, if you know your geography!"

**Northern Summer Southern Winter**     **Northern Winter Southern Summer**

Sun's rays

### REASONS FOR SEASONS

Earth is a slightly tilted planet. Its axis doesn't point straight up and down in space, but leans over a little. For part of the year, the North Pole leans toward the Sun. This brings more sunshine and summer to the northern half of the planet. Six months later, when Earth is halfway around its orbit, the South Pole is tipped toward the Sun, bringing summer to the southern half of the world.

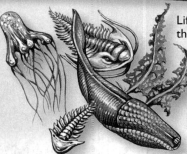

Life abounds in the oceans.

### 550 MILLION YEARS AGO

Hundreds of plant and animal species evolve in the oceans. Most die out, but a few of these strange early creatures evolve into fish and shellfish. Amphibians develop later and crawl onto land.

### 228 MILLION YEARS AGO

New reptile-like creatures walk on two hind legs across the land. These early dinosaurs evolve to rule Earth for 160 million years.

First dinosaurs appear.

### 200,000 YEARS AGO

The dinosaurs are long gone, and mammals now rule the world. The first modern humans appear.

First humans appear.

# Our Moon

IMAGINE WALKING ON the Moon. The Moon is about one-quarter the size of Earth and has only one-sixth as much gravity. You would weigh six times less on the Moon. That means you could jump six times higher than on Earth and bound around in giant leaps like a kangaroo.

There is one catch. You can't go outside without wearing a spacesuit. The Moon has absolutely no air. There's no oxygen to breathe. No liquid water. No plants. No life of any kind. Your spacesuit supplies everything you need to survive. It also keeps you at a comfortable temperature. In the sunshine, the Moon's surface can be as hot as boiling water, at 212°F (100°C). At night, temperatures can plunge to –240°F (–150°C). And lunar nights last two weeks.

After your moonwalk, you can admire your footprints in the powdery surface. With no wind or rain to wipe them away, they will still be there millions of years from now.

**INSIDE THE MOON**

- Rocky crust
- Rocky mantle
- Molten zone
- Core

## INSIDE STORY

### Moonwalking

The Moon is the only world beyond Earth that people have visited. In six Apollo missions from 1969 to 1972, 12 astronauts walked on the lunar surface. Here are some of their impressions.

*Neil Armstrong, Apollo 11:* "It has a stark beauty all its own."
*Buzz Aldrin, Apollo 11:* "Magnificent desolation."
*Alan Bean, Apollo 12:* "You can jump up in the air!"
*Pete Conrad, Apollo 12:* "Whee! Up one crater and over another. Does that look as good as it feels?"
*John Young, Apollo 16:* "Oh, look at all those beautiful rocks!"
*Charlie Duke, Apollo 16:* "Hot dawg, is this great! That first step on the lunar surface is super!"

## HANDS ON

### Phasing the Moon

You can create the phases of the Moon. All you need is a dark room, a flashlight for the Sun, a basketball covered in aluminum foil for the Moon, and two friends.

Stand in the middle of the room to represent Earth. One friend stands a few steps in front of you with the basketball Moon held high. The other friend stands a few steps behind the Moon friend and shines the flashlight Sun on the ball all the time. As the friend with the Moon circles around you, you'll see how the Moon's phases occur.

**MAPPING THE MOON**
Spacecraft are once again exploring the Moon. In 1998, NASA placed the tiny Lunar Prospector robot probe in orbit around the Moon. It discovered ice at the north and south poles of the Moon. But you can't skate on this ice, because it is mixed in with the lunar rock and soil. One day, when people return to the Moon, they may tap this ice for water and rocket fuel.

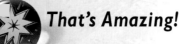

## Word Builders

The Moon is covered with **maria** and **craters**. Maria is a Latin word that means "seas." But the maria on the Moon have never been filled with water. They are actually flat plains of ancient lava. The pits that pockmark the Moon were blasted out by the impacts of comets and asteroids. These are called craters from the Greek word *krater*, meaning "bowl."

## That's Amazing!

• The Moon has the same amount of surface area as Earth's continent of Africa.
• The crater Copernicus is twice as deep as Arizona's Grand Canyon.
• In the Moon's sky, Earth appears 4 times bigger and 60 times brighter than the Moon ever does from Earth.

## Pathfinder

• Which sport have people played on the Moon? Go to pages 12–13.
• Why does the Moon sometimes look red? Go to page 29.
• Which is bigger—the Moon or Pluto? Go to page 42.

## THE NEAR SIDE OF THE MOON

This side of the Moon always faces Earth. It is marked by hundreds of thousands of craters. Apollo astronauts explored the near side of the Moon at six landing sites.

MARE FRIGORIS
(Sea of Cold)

Plato

Aristoteles

Endymion

Hercules

SINUS IRIDUM
(Bay of Rainbows)

Montes Alpes
(Alps)

Montes Caucasus
(Caucasus Mountains)

MARE IMBRIUM
(Sea of Showers)

Aristillus

Posidonius

OCEANUS PROCELLARUM
(Ocean of Storms)

Aristarchus

Archimedes

Autolycus

Apollo 15

MARE SERENITATIS
(Sea of Serenity)

Apollo 17

Cleomedes

MARE CRISIUM
(Sea of Crises)

Montes Apenninus
(Apennines)

Eratosthenes

MARE VAPORUM
(Sea of Vapors)

Kepler

Copernicus

Grimaldi

Apollo 12

Apollo 14

Ptolemaeus

Apollo 11

TRANQUILLITATIS
(Sea of Tranquillity)

MARE FECUNDITATIS
(Sea of Fertility)

Langrenus

MARE COGNITUM
(Sea of Knowledge)

Albategnius

Apollo 16

Theophilus

Gassendi

Alphonsus

MARE NECTARIS
(Sea of Nectar)

MARE HUMORUM
(Sea of Moisture)

MARE NUBIUM
(Sea of Clouds)

Rupes Recta
(Straight Wall)

Rupes Altai
(Altai Scarp)

Petavius

Tycho

Clavius

*Lunokhod 1, 1970–1971*

## WHERE DID THE MOON COME FROM?

The Moon had a smashing beginning. About four and one-half billion years ago, a small planet crashed into the young Earth. The impact ripped apart the intruder planet and blasted huge chunks of Earth's upper layers into space. The rocky debris from the intruder planet and Earth fell back together to form the Moon.

## PHASES OF THE MOON

The Moon appears to change its shape because as it travels around us, different amounts of the face we see are lit by the Sun. When the Moon comes between us and the Sun, the near side of the Moon—the side that faces us—is dark. This phase is called New Moon. Two weeks later, the Moon has moved halfway around its orbit. Now the near side is completely lit by the Sun and we see a Full Moon. The Moon takes just over 29 days to go from New Moon to New Moon.

**New Moon**
The side of the Moon facing us is dark. This phase is invisible.

**Waxing Crescent**
You can see this phase in the western evening sky just after New Moon.

**First Quarter**
Look high in the evening sky as the Sun sets in the west.

**Waxing Gibbous**
This Moon is in the early evening sky 9 to 12 days after New Moon.

**Full Moon**
This bright Moon rises in the east just as the Sun sets in the west.

**Waning Gibbous**
A few days after Full Moon, this Moon rises late at night.

**Last Quarter**
This Moon rises after midnight. It is high in the sky at dawn.

**Waning Crescent**
Get up early to see this Moon. It is low in the east at dawn.

*Apollo, Greek Sun god*     *Amaterasu, Japanese Sun god*     *Horus, Egyptian Sun god*

# The Sun

THE SUN IS a star like those we see at night, but it is much closer to us. Without the Sun nearby, Earth would be as cold and lifeless as Pluto. Plants need sunlight to grow, and people and other animals need plants to survive.

The heat of the Sun also creates our weather. It powers the winds and evaporates water to make clouds and rain. Scientists think that even slight changes in the Sun's energy may warm or cool Earth's climate.

The Sun has been shining for five billion years. How does it make so much energy? With a surface as hot as 11,000°F (6,000°C), it looks as if the Sun is on fire, but it isn't burning in the same way as a piece of wood or a lump of coal. The Sun is actually a giant nuclear-fusion bomb. Deep in its superhot core, it smashes 600 million tons of hydrogen atoms together every second, turning them into heavier helium atoms. The energy released by this atom smashing escapes into space as light and heat.

**NATURE'S LIGHT SHOW**
Storms on the Sun blow a wind of particles into space. The particles sometimes rain down onto Earth's atmosphere and, like an electric current, zap the air, causing a colored glow called an aurora. If you live in Canada, the northern United States, or Europe, or in southern Australia or New Zealand, you can often see auroras in the sky. They look like rippling curtains of green, red, or pink light.

**INSIDE THE SUN**
- Photosphere
- Convective zone
- Radiative zone
- Hydrogen core

WARNING: Never look directly at the Sun—you could go permanently blind. If you want to watch a solar eclipse, you can buy the special filters you need to use at a science center or planetarium.

## INSIDE STORY

### Ancient Sunrise

You are one of hundreds of people gathered within a circle of giant standing stones called Stonehenge, in England. It is dawn on a quiet summer morning. There are no clocks or calendars, because the year is 1500 BC. Yet everyone knows that something special is about to happen. And there it is—the Sun is rising over a special stone in the distance. It does this only on one day a year—June 21, the summer solstice. Stonehenge, your giant stone calendar, is telling you the date.

*Incan Sun mask*     *Mayan Sun temple*

## Word Builders

The Roman goddess of the dawn was named Aurora. In the Northern Hemisphere, aurora displays are known as **aurora borealis,** which means "northern dawn." In the Southern Hemisphere, people call them **aurora australis,** meaning "southern dawn."

## That's Amazing!

• In one second, the Sun sends out more energy than humans have consumed in all of recorded history.
• If you drove a car at highway speeds from Earth to the Sun, it would take 170 years to complete your journey.

## Pathfinder

• Which other probe has looked at the Sun? Go to page 17.
• How does the Sun's gravity affect the planets? Go to pages 22–23.
• Is the Sun the only star with planets? Go to pages 50–51.
• Where is the Sun in our galaxy? Go to pages 56–57.

## SPOTS ON THE SUN'S FACE

The Sun sometimes breaks out in spots. Within these dark blemishes, strong magnetic fields stop the Sun's gas from boiling and bubbling. The trapped gas cools and appears dark compared to the brilliant disc of the Sun. Scientists know that the number of sunspots peaks every 11 years, but they do not know how this cycle on the Sun affects Earth.

## SOLAR WATCHDOGS

Satellites are constantly watching our star, the Sun. The Solar and Heliospheric Observatory (SOHO), shown here, has snapped thousands of Sun pictures. Other solar spacecraft include the Wind and the Advanced Composition Explorer (ACE) satellites, which sample the particles streaming from the Sun. A satellite called Polar keeps an eye on auroras.

## GREAT BALL OF FIRE

The Sun is big—it contains 99.99 percent of all the matter in the solar system. You could pack a million Earths inside the Sun. In this image taken by the SOHO satellite, you can see a tongue of gas called a prominence shooting into space. Earth would be the size of a pinhead beside this giant prominence.

## ECLIPSE SHADOWPLAY

### SOLAR ECLIPSE

A total eclipse of the Sun is spectacular. Once every one or two years, the Moon comes directly between us and the Sun. Its shadow falls in a narrow band across Earth. People in this band see the Moon's dark disc cover the Sun for a few minutes. Only the faint outer atmosphere of the Sun, called the corona, remains visible.

**Eclipse of the Sun**

Earth

Moon

Sun's rays

**Eclipse of the Moon**

Moon

Earth

Sun's rays

### LUNAR ECLIPSE

A total eclipse of the Moon can be seen over the entire night side of Earth. When the Full Moon passes through the dark inner part of Earth's shadow, the Moon goes dark for an hour or more. Sunlight filtering through our atmosphere turns the eclipsed Moon deep red.

# Mercury and Venus

WELCOME TO THE solar system's hottest planets. Mercury and Venus both orbit much closer to the Sun's warmth than Earth does. But that's where any similarity between Mercury and Venus ends.

Mercury, the innermost planet, rushes around the Sun every 88 days. But it takes about two-thirds of that time—59 Earth days—just to spin around once on its axis. Its long day and short year combine so that sunrises occur 176 Earth days apart. At midday on Mercury, look for shade—temperatures soar to 800°F (430°C). At night, bundle up—the thermometer plunges to –290°F (–180°C).

There's no way to escape the heat on Venus, which is even hotter than Mercury. Everywhere, day and night, the temperature is a searing 860°F (460°C). That's hot enough to melt lead, tin, and zinc. Venus suffers from a greenhouse effect gone wild. A thick atmosphere of carbon dioxide traps solar energy and heats up Venus in the same way that a thick blanket keeps you warm at night. What's worse, acid rain falls from its clouds of sulfuric acid. Venus is a tough place to land a spacecraft. From 1970 to 1986, the Russian space program landed ten Venera probes on the surface of Venus. None of them lasted for more than an hour before malfunctioning.

### INSIDE MERCURY

— Rocky crust
— Rocky mantle
— Iron/nickel core

### INSIDE VENUS

— Rocky crust
— Rocky mantle
— Iron/nickel core

## HANDS ON
## Spotting the Inner Planets

People from many lands have called Venus the evening star or morning star. Since Venus orbits near the Sun, it always appears just after the Sun sets and just before the Sun rises. If you see a dazzling object low in the sky during the early evening or morning, then that's probably Venus, outshining every other star and planet. Venus shines brightly because its thick clouds reflect the Sun's light.

Mercury is so near the Sun that it always appears just above the horizon, which makes it hard to see. In this photo, Mercury is lost in the tree branches, while Venus is the bright dot at the top of the photo.

### VENUSIAN VOLCANOES

This image from the Magellan space probe shows Maat Mons, the highest of the 167 giant volcanoes on Venus. Maat Mons towers 26,000 feet (8,000 m) above the Venusian plains, so it is nearly as tall as Mount Everest. Maat Mons gradually built up over millions of years as lava poured from its summit. No one knows whether Venus's volcanoes still erupt.

### THE CLOUDY PLANET

Imagine yourself on Venus. The air around you is clear, but it shimmers in the intense heat. It's a dull day, like a heavily overcast day on Earth. The sky looks red and is covered completely by a smooth, dense haze. From Venus, you can never see the Sun during the day nor the stars at night.

Rocket thrusters

Solar panels

Spacecraft turns to beam data to Earth.

Main antenna

Sulfuric acid clouds

### MAPPING A NEW WORLD

How do you map a planet always covered in clouds? From 1989 to 1993, NASA's Magellan probe beamed radar signals at the surface of Venus. The radio waves passed through the clouds, hit the surface, and bounced back to Magellan. Using the bounced-back radio waves, the probe helped create a picture of Venus's surface.

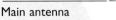

Radar signals are sent to Venus.

Surface of Venus

## Word Builders

• **Mercury** moves so quickly around the Sun that the Romans named it for the swift messenger of their gods, Mercurius.
• **Venus** is named for the Roman goddess of love and beauty. The planet was also called Ishtar by the Sumerians, Kukulkán by the Mayans, and Quetzalcoatl by the Aztecs.

## That's Amazing!

• Mercury's dense core of iron and nickel is larger than our Moon.
• One impact feature on Mercury—Caloris Basin—is so big that it would stretch halfway across North America.
• Venus spins backward compared to all the other planets except Uranus. Perhaps a giant asteroid hit Venus and flipped it upside down.

## Pathfinder

• Saturn's moon Titan is cloudy like Venus. How will scientists look at its surface? Go to page 17.
• Where are Mercury and Venus in the solar system? Go to pages 22–23.
• Does Mercury really look like the Moon? Go to pages 26–27.

### THE CRATERED PLANET

Mercury looks like the Moon. Both are airless worlds covered with craters. Unlike the Moon, Mercury seems to lack any large lava plains. But we haven't seen all of Mercury close-up. Because of its flight path, Mariner 10, the only spacecraft to visit Mercury, could map only half the planet.

### STRIPS OF VENUS

Magellan transmitted its radio pictures back to Earth. Each picture revealed a strip of Venus 10,000 miles (16,000 km) long from north to south but only 15 miles (24 km) wide. Mission scientists then pieced together the narrow strips into a map of Venus.

Data are received on Earth.

Data are sent to mission control.

Data are downloaded into computer.

Deep-space tracking antenna

Scientist adds new data to map.

The completed map of Venus

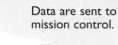

# Mars

MARS IS THE planet most like Earth. A day on Mars is just 40 minutes longer than a day on Earth. Like Earth, Mars has seasons of summer and winter. And billions of years ago, Mars was almost as warm as Earth. Rivers flowed across the land. An ocean might have covered half the planet, and primitive life could have flourished. In 1996, scientists announced they had found fossils of bacteria, a simple form of life, inside a meteorite from Mars. Some scientists disagree with this claim. They think we have yet to find proof of life on Mars.

During your lifetime, astronauts will probably visit Mars. If you were one of these astronauts, you could walk around easily on Mars's dusty, red surface. You would need a spacesuit, though, because the air on Mars contains no oxygen, just carbon dioxide.

Your spacesuit would also keep you warm. On a summer day, Martian temperatures reach only 32°F (0°C), the freezing point of water, but at night they plunge to –110°F (–80°C), as cold as Antarctica in winter. During winter on Mars, prepare for bone-chilling temperatures colder than any place on Earth, about –190°F (–125°C). This is so cold that the air at the north and south poles of Mars freezes into caps of carbon dioxide ice.

## INSIDE MARS

- Rocky crust
- Rocky mantle
- Iron core

## CANYON DEEP, MOUNTAIN HIGH

Mars is a planet of towering volcanoes and gaping canyons. The tallest volcano is Olympus Mons. You would need to stack three Mount Everests on top of each other to reach the summit of this massive mountain. The longest canyon is Valles Marineris. Placed on Earth, Valles Marineris would stretch across North America. Arizona's Grand Canyon would be a scratch beside this mighty gash in the Martian crust.

*Map labels: VASTITA, ARCADIA PLANITIA, Alba Fossae, Alba Patera, Olympus Mons, AMAZONIS PLANITIA, Ascraeus Mons, Pavonis Mons, DAEDALIA PLANUM, Arsia Mons, Tharsis Montes, SYRI PLANU, TERRA CIMMERIA, TERRA SIRENUM, PLANU*

Chasma = long depression (like a canyon)
Mons = mountain
Montes = mountains
Fossae = long, shallow depressions (like grooves)
Patera = irregular or complex crater
Planitia = low plain
Planum = plateau or plain
Terra = extensive landmass
Tholus = small mountain or hill
Vallis, Valles = valley
Vastitas = extensive plain

## MARTIAN MOONS

Two little moons dart around Mars. Deimos, the outer moon, is only 9 miles (15 km) long, no bigger than a small city. Phobos, the inner moon, is a potato-shaped world 17 miles (27 km) long. Both moons may be ancient asteroids captured into orbit by Mars's gravity early in its history.

Deimos

Phobos

## INSIDE STORY

### Mission to Mars

Imagine that you are the first astronaut on a mission to Mars. You slowly climb down the ladder of your lander. The Apollo astronauts took only three days to reach the Moon, but you have endured a six-month flight to get to Mars and, because of the planet's orbit, it will be two more years before you see home again. Without Earth's atmosphere to protect you, you've been exposed to harmful radiation from space. And your muscles and bones are weak after being weightless for so long.

Now you are about to become the first human to walk on Mars. The landscape looks like a beautiful red desert. The sky is an eerie shade of orange. You step onto the red sand. Billions of people on Earth are watching you on TV and listening for your first words. What do you say?

## Word Builders

Given the red color of Mars's surface, it's not surprising that ancient people thought of blood and battles when they looked at the planet. The Babylonians called it **Nergal**, the star of death. The Greeks named it **Ares**, after their god of war. Today we know it as **Mars**, for the Roman god of war.

## That's Amazing!

• If you could melt all the ice that exists on Mars, scientists think it would form an ocean between 33 and 330 feet (10 and 100 m) deep.
• Deimos's gravity is so weak you could launch yourself off this Martian moon by running fast and taking a giant leap.

## Pathfinder

• Why did NASA send a rover to Mars? Go to pages 16–17.
• What did the bacteria-like markings in the Martian meteorite look like? Go to page 19.
• Are Phobos and Deimos like asteroids? Go to pages 34–35.

The Face, as photographed by Viking 1

The Face, as photographed by Global Surveyor

### THE CASE OF THE FACE

In 1976, the Viking 1 orbiter photographed a mysterious feature that looked like a face. Was this evidence for life on Mars? In 1998, the Mars Global Surveyor probe photographed the feature with a much better camera. The sharp new images exposed the truth. The Face is really an eroded hill sculpted by winds, not by Martians.

### INVADERS FROM MARS!

Could Martians conquer Earth? In 1897, H. G. Wells wrote the science-fiction novel *The War of the Worlds* about a Martian invasion of Earth. A 1938 radio broadcast of the story scared thousands of people into thinking that Martians were really invading. We now know that Mars is too cold and its air is too thin to support advanced life. Martians do not exist.

Illustration from *The War of the Worlds*

## MARS ON EARTH

So far, no astronauts have been to Mars, and no robot probes have returned with samples of Martian rocks. Yet scientists think they have found more than a dozen pieces of Mars on Earth. Here's how the rocks may have got here.

### TAKEOFF

A small asteroid smashes into Mars. The force of the impact makes a crater and blasts pieces of Mars into space.

### IN SPACE

Like a flurry of small asteroids, these Martian rocks go into orbit around the Sun for millions of years.

### TO EARTH

Eventually some of the rocks collide with Earth. The rocks fall to the ground as meteorites. One particular Martian meteorite lands thousands of years ago.

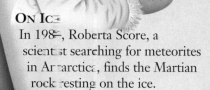

### ON ICE

In 1984, Roberta Score, a scientist searching for meteorites in Antarctica, finds the Martian rock resting on the ice.

# Asteroids and Meteoroids

BETWEEN MARS AND Jupiter lies a region known as the asteroid belt. It contains tens of thousands of asteroids, but they are so far apart that you could fly through the belt and never see a single asteroid from your spaceship window. Almost all asteroids stay in the belt, but Trojan asteroids are farther out, in the same path around the Sun as Jupiter. Near-Earth asteroids wander close to the Sun and occasionally cross the orbit of Earth.

Astronomers think that asteroids are lumps of rock and metal left over from the early days of the solar system. The pull from Jupiter's gravity would have stopped the lumps from smashing together to form a planet. The largest asteroid, Ceres, is nearly as big as Texas in the United States, but most asteroids are the size of mountains.

Throughout the solar system, countless small rocks known as meteoroids orbit the Sun. The bigger chunks are usually pieces of asteroids shattered by collisions in the asteroid belt. The smaller specks are mostly dust particles shed by passing comets. Our planet collides with thousands of these meteoroids every day.

## INSIDE STORY

### Hunting for Asteroids

"It was a cold night in December 1997 at the Spacewatch Telescope in Arizona," describes Jim Scotti. "I was alone in the dome when one asteroid appeared on the computer that was moving unusually fast." Jim Scotti had found a space rock called 1997 $XF_{11}$, one of about 200 asteroids known to come dangerously close to Earth. "Though the excitement of finding our first near-Earth asteroids has worn off, it's still satisfying to bag a new one."

### WHAT A WHOPPER!
Sometimes chunks of space rock survive their fiery fall through the atmosphere and land on Earth. These are called meteorites. Most meteorites would fit in your pocket, but some are much larger. This meteorite is almost as big as a baby elephant. It was recovered from Greenland in 1897.

### SHOOTING STARS
When a tiny meteoroid comes too close to Earth, it burns up high in our atmosphere. The burning meteoroid creates a brief streak of light in the sky. People often call this streak a shooting star, but the correct name for the streak is a meteor.

## Word Builders

An astronomer who discovers an asteroid gets to name it. Many asteroids, such as Ceres, Pallas, and Juno, have been named for mythological figures. Some are named for famous astronomers. Four are named John, Paul, George, and Ringo, after the Beatles rock group. One is even named Mr. Spock after an astronomer's cat—and TV science-fiction character.

## That's Amazing!

• Squeezing together all our solar system's asteroids would make a world about one-third the size of our Moon.
• The biggest meteorite ever found, the Hoba West meteorite in Namibia, Africa, is about 8 feet (2.5 m) long and weighs 66 tons (60 metric tons)—that's as heavy as nine elephants!

## Pathfinder

• What other rovers have explored space? Go to pages 16–17.
• Where do asteroids orbit? Go to pages 22–23.
• When can you see a meteor shower? Go to page 44.

## REALLY DEEP IMPACT

Every few million years, a giant piece of space rock collides with Earth. This happened 65 million years ago when something as wide as a city—a large asteroid or a comet—smashed into what is now the Yucatán Peninsula of Mexico. The results were disastrous for dinosaurs, but some reptiles, birds, and mammals survived.

### GIANT SPACE ROCKS

Most asteroids probably look like this one, called Ida. In 1993, while on its way to Jupiter, the Galileo probe took this photo of Ida. The space rock is 33 miles (53 km) long, about as big as New York City in the United States. The probe discovered that Ida has its own moon, which is 1 mile (1.6 km) wide. Astronomers named the tiny moon Dactyl, after the creatures in Greek mythology who lived on Mount Ida.

### DRIVING ON AN ASTEROID

In 2003, scientists plan to send the MUSES-C spacecraft to Nereus, a near-Earth asteroid that is less than 1 mile (1.6 km) wide. The spacecraft will carry a nanorover—a rover 10 times lighter than the one that went to Mars. The nanorover will roll and hop over the asteroid's surface and snap close-up pictures of rocks and soil. Meanwhile, the MUSES-C lander will fire explosive bullets into Nereus, collect the asteroid bits blown off by the explosions, and return them to Earth for scientists to study.

### THE BIG HIT

The rocky asteroid—or icy comet—slams into Earth. Exploding with the force of 100 million hydrogen bombs, it blasts a crater 100 miles (160 km) wide.

### A HOT TIME

Gigantic waves swamp the region that is now the Caribbean and the United States. Fiery debris blown upward by the explosion rains back to Earth and sparks worldwide forest fires.

### A LONG DARK NIGHT

Fine ash and soot from the impact linger high in the air for months, blocking the Sun. Many plants die, followed by the animals that eat them. With fewer prey, meat-eating animals die, too. The Age of Dinosaurs is over.

# Jupiter

VISITING JUPITER IN person would be hard to do. For one thing, you'd need a spaceship built like a balloon because there's no place to land. The biggest of all the planets, Jupiter is one huge ball of hydrogen and helium gases. These same gases make up the Sun, but Jupiter would need to contain 80 times more gas before it could shine like a star.

You'd also need to watch out for Jupiter's wild weather. Despite its size, this giant spins faster than any other planet—a day on Jupiter is less than 10 hours long. Jupiter's speedy spin helps whip the clouds into storms as big as a continent on Earth. Winds rage at up to 300 miles per hour (500 km/h). Superbolts of lightning crackle in the thunderclouds.

In 1995, the Galileo spacecraft started to orbit Jupiter, taking hundreds of pictures of the planet's storms, moons, and its faint, dusty ring. Galileo also sent a capsule, known as the Probe, into Jupiter's churning atmosphere.

## TAKING THE PLUNGE

On December 7, 1995, the Galileo spacecraft's cone-shaped Probe plunged into Jupiter's atmosphere at 50 times the speed of a bullet. Powerful winds blew the Probe hundreds of miles sideways as it descended through clouds of ammonia ice crystals. For an hour, its instruments sniffed and sampled the air, until Jupiter's fierce atmosphere first crushed and then vaporized the Probe.

## INSIDE JUPITER

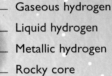

— Gaseous hydrogen
— Liquid hydrogen
— Metallic hydrogen
— Rocky core

## COMET CRASH

In July 1994, 21 pieces of Comet Shoemaker-Levy 9 slammed into Jupiter one after the other. Telescopes around the world watched as the explosions scarred Jupiter's cloud tops with black spots as big as Earth. Months passed before Jupiter returned to normal.

Diameter: 2,256 miles (3,630 km)

Diameter: 1,951 miles (3,140 km)

## JUPITER'S GIANT MOONS

Jupiter's powerful gravity controls a family of 16 moons. Twelve are the size of small asteroids—and some might actually be asteroids captured by Jupiter's gravity long ago. But four of Jupiter's moons are bigger than Pluto. The astronomer Galileo discovered these four giant moons in 1610. People still call them the Galilean satellites.

## FIERY IO

Io is a world of volcanoes. Io's volcanoes not only erupt with molten rock, but they also pour liquid sulfur over the surface. The sulfur cools and hardens into a wildly colored crust of yellows, oranges, and reds. Some people think that this moon looks like a pizza.

## Word Builders

Jupiter and its moons are called the **Jovian** system. **Jove** was another name for Jupiter, ruler of the Roman gods. If people are jovial, they are happy and fun-loving, like Jove himself. Most of the planet's moons are named after the god's many wives.

## That's Amazing!

• Hurricanes on Earth last about two weeks. Jupiter's Great Red Spot has been raging for at least 300 years.
• Lightning bolts on Jupiter are 10 times more powerful than those on Earth.
• Metis, the innermost moon of Jupiter, zips around the planet so quickly that it could cross North America in just 2.5 minutes.

## Pathfinder

• The astronomer Galileo found Jupiter's four large moons. What else did he discover? Go to page 10.
• What do scientists hope to find in Europa's ocean? Go to pages 18–19.
• What did Comet Shoemaker-Levy 9 look like? Go to page 45.

### STRIPES AND SPOTS

Everywhere you look on Jupiter, you see clouds. There are white clouds of ammonia, blue clouds of water, and brown clouds of sulfur compounds. Jupiter's rapid spin wraps these clouds into long stripes around the planet. The Great Red Spot spins like a hurricane in the clouds. This giant storm system is big enough to swallow two Earths. Astronomers are still trying to work out how the spot formed.

Jupiter photographed by Voyager 2

Great Red Spot photographed by the Galileo spacecraft

### FLOATING IN THE CLOUDS

Imagine floating in Jupiter's atmosphere, where clouds come in a rainbow of colors. This image, taken by the Galileo spacecraft, has been processed in a computer. It shows what you would see if you were in between Jupiter's cloud layers.

## HANDS ON
### Following the Moons

To find Jupiter's four giant moons, you first need to find Jupiter. Call your local planetarium or science center, or check a web site such as *www.skypub.com*. Once you know where to look, you should be able to spot Jupiter by eye. Then you can use a pair of binoculars to find the moons, which look like tiny points of light. The moons move around Jupiter, so if you look again on another night, you'll see that they have shifted position. Sometimes a moon goes behind Jupiter, and you won't be able to see it at all. The pictures below show the positions of the moons on two different nights.

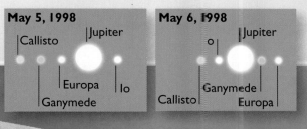

May 5, 1998 — Callisto, Jupiter, Europa, Io, Ganymede

May 6, 1998 — Jupiter, Callisto, Ganymede, Europa

### ICY EUROPA

The Voyager 1 and 2 and Galileo spacecraft discovered that Europa is completely covered with a crust of ice. Below the ice may lurk a dark ocean of liquid water—perhaps the only other ocean in the solar system beyond Earth.

### GIGANTIC GANYMEDE

Ganymede is so big that if it orbited the Sun instead of Jupiter, we would call it a planet. The biggest moon in the solar system, Ganymede is more than twice as large as Pluto and a bit larger than Mercury.

Diameter: 3,269 miles (5,260 km)

### CRATERED CALLISTO

Thousands of craters pepper Callisto's icy surface. Apart from the occasional impact of a comet, this cold moon has hardly changed for billions of years.

Diameter: 2,983 miles (4,800 km)

# Saturn

IF YOU COULD approach Saturn, the most impressive sight would be the thousands of rings that circle the planet. Remove its rings and Saturn would look like a smaller version of Jupiter. Saturn is also a giant planet made of hydrogen and helium gases. It spins quickly, too, with a day lasting 10 hours and 40 minutes Earth time.

On closer inspection, you'd notice that Saturn's bands of clouds are less colorful than the clouds on Jupiter. This is probably because Saturn is farther from the Sun—and colder. Temperatures in Saturn's clouds of ammonia ice crystals hover at –210°F (–135°C). Winds blow even more strongly on Saturn than on Jupiter. In some places, Saturn's winds roar at 800 miles per hour (1,300 km/h), 11 times faster than a hurricane on Earth.

If you traveled around Saturn, you could count 18 moons. The giant is Titan, the second-largest moon in the solar system and the only one with a thick atmosphere. You wouldn't be able to see through Titan's dense, orange clouds, but in 2004 the Cassini spacecraft will send a probe plunging to its surface.

## INSIDE STORY
## The Planet with Ears

The year is 1656. Christiaan Huygens invites you to look through his telescope. It makes objects appear 50 times bigger. "You see what I have discovered?" asks Huygens. "Saturn is surrounded by a thin flat ring nowhere touching the planet." Wow! You *can* see the rings. Saturn had puzzled earlier observers, including Galileo, Fontana, and Riccioli, but their telescopes were so poor, Saturn looked like it had "handles" or "ears." Today, most backyard telescopes clearly show Saturn's rings.

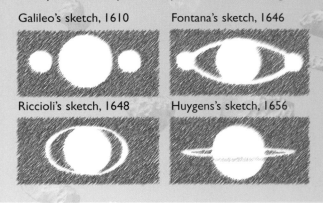

Galileo's sketch, 1610     Fontana's sketch, 1646

Riccioli's sketch, 1648     Huygens's sketch, 1656

**INSIDE SATURN**

— Gaseous hydrogen
— Liquid hydrogen
— Metallic hydrogen
— Rocky core

— A Ring
— Cassini's Division
— B Ring
— C Ring

**SCARFACE**
A giant crater scars Mimas, a small inner moon of Saturn. Millions of years ago, a large object crashed into Mimas and carved out this crater. If the object had been any larger, it would have smashed the little moon into pieces. Mimas and most of Saturn's other moons are named after members of the Titans, a family of Greek supergods ruled by the giant Titan.

**RING WORLD**
Three main sets of rings orbit Saturn. The outer A Ring is separated from the B Ring by a dark gap called Cassini's Division, first seen by Giovanni Cassini in 1675. This gap is as wide as North America. The inner C Ring is darker than the others because it contains fewer ice particles to reflect sunlight.

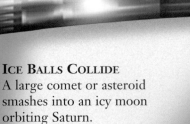

**ICE BALLS COLLIDE**
A large comet or asteroid smashes into an icy moon orbiting Saturn.

## RUNNING RINGS AROUND SATURN

The rings of Saturn remain among the most beautiful yet mysterious objects in the solar system. How did the rings get there? And when did they form? One theory suggests the rings are only a few million years old and were formed by a cosmic collision. This is how it might have happened.

## Word Builders

If you like **Saturdays**, you can thank Saturn. The day is named after the sixth planet, which was named after the Roman god of the harvest. It's easy to tell what objects **Sunday** (Sun-day) and **Monday** (Moon-day) are named after. But the other days? They're named after gods from Norse legends—Tiw **(Tuesday)**, Woden **(Wednesday)**, Thor **(Thursday)**, and Frigg **(Friday)**.

## That's Amazing!

• Saturn's rings are no thicker than a six-story building. If you wanted to build a scale model, you'd need a sheet of paper eight city blocks wide but only as thick as a page in this book.
• Saturn would float on water—if you could find a big enough ocean!

## Pathfinder

• How will scientists land a probe on Saturn's moon Titan? Go to page 17.
• Is there life on any of Saturn's moons? Go to pages 18–19
• What other planets have rings? Go to pages 36–37 and 40–41.

## INSIDE THE BLIZZARD

Saturn's rings are a blizzard of snowballs. From a distance, the rings look solid, but from close-up, you would see they are made of billions of ice chunks the size of hailstones and snowballs. If you could pack all the ring particles together, you could make a single giant snowball about 60 miles (100 km) across—the size of a small moon of Saturn.

## SNOWY SMITHEREENS

The impact shatters the moon into a cloud of icy particles. These particles then orbit Saturn like a swarm of moonlets.

## SPREADING OUT

Constant collisions among the icy particles grind most of them into even smaller pieces. Over the years, these particles spread out to form a broad ring around the planet.

## SHEPHERD MOONS

Some of the icy particles that were not ground up remain as small moons that skim near the edge of the rings. Like sheep dogs herding a flock of sheep, the gravity of these shepherd moons keeps the ring particles in their places.

# Uranus and Neptune

FOR THOUSANDS OF years, people thought the most distant planet was Saturn. Then, in 1781, William Herschel saw what he called a "curious nebulous star or perhaps a comet" through his telescope. He later realized it was the seventh planet, Uranus. Tiny wobbles in the path of Uranus led astronomers to look for a more distant planet that might be tugging at Uranus. Johann Galle and Heinrich D'Arrest spotted Neptune, the eighth planet, in 1846.

If you visited Uranus and Neptune, you'd find that in many ways they are like twins. Both are four times bigger than Earth. Each is circled by dark, thin rings and has an atmosphere choked with poisonous methane gas. This gas soaks up red light but scatters blue light back into space, making Uranus and Neptune look blue-green. Dive beneath the atmosphere and you'd discover a thick, slushy layer of ice and water.

Uranus and Neptune do have their differences. If you kept going past Neptune's slushy layer, you might come to a hot core. Astronomers think heat from this core rises, stirs up the cloud tops, and unleashes strong winds and large storms. The weather in Uranus's atmosphere seems calm by comparison. At the center of Uranus, you'd probably find a cold core.

### THE VIEW FROM TRITON

Ringed Neptune looms large in the sky of Triton, the largest of Neptune's eight moons. Temperatures on Triton plunge to –390°F (–235°C). That's as cold as any moon or planet in the solar system. Despite the deep freeze, Triton's surface is dotted with geysers that spew out dark jets of supercold nitrogen ice and gas.

**INSIDE URANUS**
— Hydrogen, helium, and methane gases
— Water, ammonia, and methane slush
— Rocky core

**INSIDE NEPTUNE**
— Hydrogen, helium, and methane gases
— Water, ammonia, and methane slush
— Rocky core

Sun
Neptune
Jupiter
Voyager 2
Uranus
Saturn
Voyager 1

### INTERPLANETARY TRAVELER

Much of what we know about the four gas giant planets—Jupiter, Saturn, Uranus, and Neptune—was discovered by NASA's Voyager space probes. Launched from Earth in 1977, Voyager 1 and Voyager 2 explored Jupiter and Saturn in 1979, 1980, and 1981.

### SAIL ON, VOYAGER

Voyager 1 visited only Jupiter and Saturn. It then flew away from the solar system, its main mission over. But Voyager 2's mission was to complete a grand tour of all four gas giant planets. It sailed past Uranus in 1986 and Neptune in 1989.

## Word Builders

In 1997, astronomers discovered two new moons orbiting Uranus. They named the small moons **Sycorax** and **Caliban**, after two characters in *The Tempest*, a play by William Shakespeare. Sycorax is a witch, and Caliban is her beastly son. Most of the moons of Uranus are named for characters in Shakespeare's plays.

## That's Amazing!

• Neptune's moon Triton is the only known moon in the solar system that orbits its planet in the opposite direction from the planet's rotation.
• Because Neptune's year—the time it takes to orbit the Sun—is 164 Earth years long, no one on Earth could live to be one Neptune year old.

## Pathfinder

• What sort of missions were the Voyager missions? Go to pages 16–17.
• What are the other gas giants? Go to pages 36–37 and 38–39.
• Have other planets been found in modern times? Go to page 42.

### URANUS, THE SIDEWAYS PLANET

Compared to the other planets, Uranus is tilted over on its side. For much of Uranus's year, one of its two poles points at the Sun and its rings face the Sun. One theory for this strange position is that billions of years ago a giant asteroid whacked Uranus so hard that the planet toppled over.

Diameter:
31,766 miles
(50,826 km)

### MARVELOUS MOON MIRANDA

In 1986, Voyager 2 snapped close-ups of Uranus and several of its 17 moons. The inner moon Miranda looks strange, as if it has been smashed apart by an impact and then pulled back together by gravity into a jumble of icy blocks.

Diameter:
75 miles (120 km)

### INSIDE STORY

## Discovering the Rings

You're part of a team of astronomers flying on the Kuiper Airborne Observatory. A telescope pokes through the side of the airplane. Your target tonight—on March 10, 1977—is Uranus. You watch as a star is about to disappear behind the planet. An astronomer calls out, "Okay. We got one. We got a blip here." A colleague confirms the readings. "We got blips again. They're real." Something is causing the star to wink out just before it passes behind Uranus. "There's no clouds," someone reports. "Well, maybe this is a ring of Uranus. Hey, there's another one!" Your team has discovered something exciting—rings around Uranus—the first rings ever seen around a planet other than Saturn.

### TRACKING THE GREAT DARK SPOT

Voyager 2 photographed the Great Dark Spot, a storm on Neptune as big as Earth. Scientists tracked this giant storm for many days. Five years later, when astronomers used the Hubble Space Telescope to look at Neptune again, the Great Dark Spot had disappeared.

### HELLO FROM PLANET EARTH

Both Voyager 1 and Voyager 2 are now on their way to the stars. In case aliens find them, each probe carries recorded greetings from the people of Earth. The gold-plated record cover shows the position of Earth in the Milky Way Galaxy.

# Pluto and Beyond

AT THE EDGE of the solar system lies Pluto, the smallest planet. From its cold surface, you would see the Sun as a brilliant star blazing in a black sky. Looming large in the sky is Charon, Pluto's moon. At 745 miles (1,200 km) across, Charon is half the size of Pluto. The two worlds are like a double planet dancing around the Sun. Both Pluto and Charon are made mostly of rock-hard ice.

Pluto's dim landscape is a patchwork of light, frost-covered regions and dark, frost-free regions. The frost covering is made of frozen nitrogen and methane chilled to –396°F (–238°C). The frost-free regions are a few degrees warmer. This difference in temperature stirs up cold winds in the thin nitrogen-methane air.

Astronomers once suspected that another planet orbited beyond Pluto. New calculations show that a tenth planet probably doesn't exist. But thousands of small icy comets orbit beyond Pluto, in a region called the Kuiper Belt. Some astronomers now wonder whether we should even call Pluto a planet—perhaps it really belongs to the Kuiper Belt. Instead of being the solar system's smallest planet, Pluto might be the largest object in the Kuiper Belt.

**INSIDE PLUTO**

— Water-methane-nitrogen ice
— Water ice
— Rocky core

## INSIDE STORY

### Discovering Planet X

Clyde Tombaugh discovered Pluto at 4:00 PM on February 18, 1930. The Lowell Observatory had hired Tombaugh to search for a ninth planet, known as Planet X. He photographed regions of the sky by night, and then examined each photo for unusual moving objects during the day. "Suddenly I spied a fifteenth-magnitude image popping out…. 'That's it,' I exclaimed to myself…. A terrific thrill came over me. Oh! I had better look at my watch and note the time. This would be a historic discovery." Tombaugh then walked down the hall to the office of the observatory director. "Trying to control myself, I stepped into his office as nonchalantly as possible. 'Dr. Slipher, I have found your Planet X.'"

**HELLO, PLUTO!**
Lop-eared Pluto first appeared in a 1930 cartoon. Walt Disney named Mickey Mouse's dog after the planet Pluto, which had just been discovered.

**FUZZY FACE**
Our best view of Pluto, captured by the Hubble Space Telescope, shows fuzzy dark markings and bright polar caps. We won't see sharper views until the Pluto-Kuiper Express spacecraft explore the planet in 2013.

## Word Builders

• In 1930, 11-year-old Venetia Burney of Oxford, England, suggested the new planet be named **Pluto,** for the Greek god of the underworld.
• When James Christy discovered Pluto's moon in 1978, he named it **Charon,** for the ferryman in Greek mythology who rowed souls across the River Styx to the underworld.

## That's Amazing!

• Pluto's day (one rotation of Pluto on its axis) and month (one orbit of Charon around Pluto) are the same length—six Earth days and nine hours.
• The thin atmosphere of Pluto freezes into methane snow every winter.
• Signals from the Pluto-Kuiper Express spacecraft will take nearly six hours to reach Earth from Pluto.

## Pathfinder

• Have spacecraft visited all the other planets? Go to pages 16–17.
• How big is Pluto compared to the Sun? Go to page 23.
• Pluto might look like Triton, one of Neptune's moons. What does Triton look like? Go to pages 40–41.
• What lies beyond the Kuiper Belt? Go to pages 44–45.

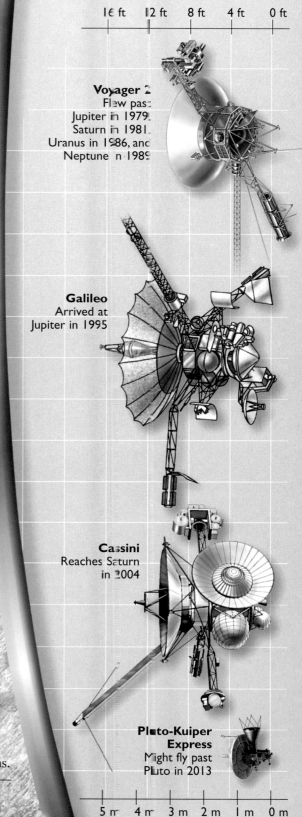

### THE SPORTS CAR PROBE

The probes that visited Jupiter, Saturn, Uranus, and Neptune were as large as trucks. A probe as heavy as these would take decades to reach Pluto. But the two Pluto-Kuiper Express spacecraft will be like fast sports cars—small and light, so a rocket can shoot them toward Pluto at high speed.

16 ft   12 ft   8 ft   4 ft   0 ft

**Voyager 2**
Flew past
Jupiter in 1979,
Saturn in 1981,
Uranus in 1986, and
Neptune in 1989

**Galileo**
Arrived at
Jupiter in 1995

**Cassini**
Reaches Saturn
in 2004

**Pluto-Kuiper Express**
Might fly past
Pluto in 2013

5 m   4 m   3 m   2 m   1 m   0 m

### MISSION TO THE LAST PLANET

No spacecraft has ever visited Pluto, but that may change if the Pluto-Kuiper Express spacecraft are launched as scheduled. In 2013, after a journey of 10 years, a small spacecraft will fly past Pluto, the reddish world in this picture, and Charon, the gray world. A second spacecraft may follow six months later. Before flying on to explore icy objects in the Kuiper Belt, each spacecraft might send a little probe crashing into Pluto.

1989

2113

Sun

Neptune

Pluto's orbit

Pluto

### ODDBALL ORBIT

All the other planets in our solar system orbit in the same flat plane, but little Pluto's orbit is tilted into a long, oval shape. For most of its 248-year orbit, Pluto is the outermost planet, but it sometimes crosses over the orbit of Neptune, making Neptune the outermost planet. From 1979 to 1999, Pluto was closer to the Sun than Neptune was. By 2113, Pluto will be at the most distant point on its orbit—more than 4.5 billion miles (7.3 billion km) from the Sun.

# Comets

MOST COMETS STAY in the deep freeze of space. Some orbit in the Kuiper Belt, just beyond Pluto. Others are farther out, in the Oort Cloud—a swarm of millions of comets that extends partway to the nearest star. Sometimes, perhaps after colliding with another comet, a comet falls out of the deep freeze and into an orbit that takes it toward the Sun.

In the deep freeze, a comet is like a dirty snowball the size of a small city. As it nears the Sun's warmth, though, the comet begins to vaporize. Jets of gas and dust erupt from the nucleus, its frozen core. The gas and dust flow away from the nucleus to form long, wispy tails. Most comets take thousands of years to complete an orbit, but a few swing by the Sun every few years or decades.

Comets have hardly changed since the solar system formed, so scientists are keen to study any clues that they might contain about the birth of the solar system. Space probes can visit comets that are approaching the Sun. In 1986, the Giotto probe flew past Comet Halley's nucleus. From 2003 to 2008, the Contour probe will visit three comets. And in 2005, Deep Space 4 will collect a piece of Comet Tempel 1 and bring it back to Earth. In 2011, the Rosetta probe will drop a lander onto Comet Wirtanen's nucleus.

## HANDS ON
## *Raining Meteors*

A meteor shower happens when Earth passes through a trail of dust from a comet. Some of the strongest meteor showers are the Perseids on August 12, the Orionids on October 22, the Leonids on November 17, and the Geminids on December 14. To observe a meteor shower, try to get away from bright lights and make yourself comfortable in a deck chair. If the Moon is not above the horizon, you could see 20 to 50 meteors in an hour. The meteors will appear to be streaming from one area of the sky—during the Geminid shower, for example, all the meteors seem to come from the constellation of Gemini.

Sun — Comet

Comet orbit

Dust tail

Tails always point away from the Sun.

Gas tail

### COMET TAILS
Many comets have two tails—one made of dust and one made of gas. The tails can be millions of miles long. The pressure of sunlight and a wind made up of solar particles push the tails away from the Sun.

## FAMOUS COMETS

### HALLEY
When comets travel close to Earth, we can see them in our sky. The famous Comet Halley appears every 75 or 76 years. It last flew past Earth in 1986 and will return again in 2061.

### HYAKUTAKE
In March 1996, a comet that no one had ever seen before swept past Earth. It was only 9 million miles (14.5 million km) away, and its gossamer tail stretched nearly halfway across the sky.

## Word Builders

If you discover a comet, it will be named after you—although you may have to share your comet with other people. Alan Hale and Thomas Bopp were scanning the sky miles apart when they discovered the same comet on the same night in 1995. Their discovery became known as **Comet Hale-Bopp.**

## That's Amazing!

• Tons of comet dust float down to Earth every day. When you clean house, a few of the dust specks you sweep up may have come from comets.
• The Great Comet of 1843 had the longest tail of any comet—it stretched from the Sun to the orbit of Mars.
• During the year it was closest to the Sun, Comet Hale-Bopp gushed 9 tons of water into space every second.

## Pathfinder

• Have other probes collected samples from space? Go to page 16.
• Are comet orbits the same shape as planet orbits? Go to pages 22–23.
• Where else can meteors come from? Go to page 34.
• What did Comet Shoemaker-Levy 9 look like when it crashed into Jupiter? Go to page 36.

## SWEEPING UP COMET DUST

If all goes as planned, a probe called Stardust will zoom through the head of Comet Wild 2 (pronounced *vilt 2*) in January 2004. A disc of spongelike material called aerogel will stick out of Stardust like a big flyswatter, ready to capture dust streaming from the comet's nucleus. In January 2006, Stardust will swing by Earth to drop a capsule containing the comet dust to scientists waiting in the Utah desert in the United States.

## INSIDE STORY

### Comet Sleuth

Astronomer Carolyn Shoemaker has found more comets than anyone else in history. She finds them by inspecting photographs taken through a telescope. Her first discovery came in 1983. "I was looking through films my husband Gene and I had taken. All of a sudden, there it was, and I knew it was a comet." Even after discovering 32 comets, each new find is a thrill. "I do try to contain myself for a while, until we find out if the comet is already known. But when I see a comet, my heart gives a big leap of joy."

### EVIL STARS

Throughout history, people have thought that comets were omens of disaster. The 900-year-old Bayeux tapestry records Comet Halley's appearance in 1066, before the Battle of Hastings in England. The Latin words say, "They are in awe of the star."

### SHOEMAKER-LEVY 9

In 1992, this comet traveled too close to the powerful gravity of Jupiter and broke into 21 pieces. Two years later, the pieces slammed into Jupiter, making dark spots on the planet.

### HALE-BOPP

One of the brightest comets of the 20th century, Hale-Bopp graced Northern Hemisphere skies in March and April of 1997. This photo clearly shows its straight, blue gas tail and curving, yellow-white dust tail.

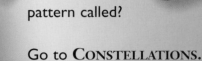

page **48** Who sees a crocodile in the stars?

What is this star pattern called?

Go to CONSTELLATIONS.

# Our Universe

BEYOND OUR SOLAR system, the universe awaits. Visit the stars and see how they change throughout their lives. Search for stars that have their own families of planets. Enter a nebula—a huge cloud of gas and dust—and witness the birth of a star. Travel past the stars in our sky and look back at the spiral arms of our galaxy, the Milky Way. Keep moving and you'll reach another galaxy—one of 50 billion in the universe. But watch out—there might be a giant black hole at the galaxy's center. Finally, end your journey at the beginning of time and discover how our amazing universe began.

page **50** How is a star born?

How do astronomers find planets around stars?

Go to SHINING STARS.

page **52** Why do stars explode?

Why do some stars regularly change their brightness?

Go to CHANGING STARS.

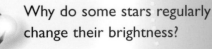

*page* **54** What is happening inside this pillar of gas?

How did this bizarre shape form?

Go to NEBULAS.

*page* **56** How is the Milky Way like a flying saucer?

What sort of galaxy is this?

Go to OUR GALAXY.

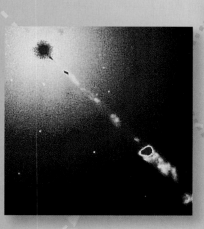

*page* **58** What is shooting out of this galaxy?

What would happen if you fell into a black hole?

Go to GALAXIES AND BLACK HOLES.

*page* **60** How did the universe begin?

How might the universe end?

Go to THE EXPANDING UNIVERSE.

# Constellations

CAN YOU SEE pictures in the stars? People have long imagined that particular groups of stars form the outlines of beasts, heroes, and gods—like dot-to-dot drawings. These star groups are called constellations. Most stars in a constellation are actually light-years apart in space—they just look close together in our sky.

Different people have imagined different pictures in the same group of stars. The ancient Greeks saw the stars of Orion as a hunter, but the Egyptians thought the same stars formed Osiris, the god of light. In China, the same stars were the warrior Tsan. The New Zealand Maoris see a canoe in Orion's stars, while an Amazon tribe sees a giant crocodile. Constellations once helped people sail ships and make calendars. Today, finding star patterns will help you learn your way around the sky.

Astronomers divide the sky into 88 constellations. Most come from Greek myths, but a few were named in modern times. You can't see all 88 constellations at once—the ones you see depend on where you live, what time of night it is, and where Earth is in its orbit around the Sun.

## NORTHERN SKY STAR CHART

If you are in the Northern Hemisphere—areas such as the United States, Canada, Europe, and Japan—these are the bright stars you can see at some time during the year. To use the map, face south and turn it so the current month is at the bottom, near you. The stars you can see in the sky are in the lower half of the map. The ones near the horizon are at the map's edge. Those overhead and behind you lie toward the map's center.

*Star chart labels:* OCTOBER, NOVEMBER, SEPTEMBER, DECEMBER, AUGUST, JANUARY, JULY, FEBRUARY, JUNE, MARCH, MAY, APRIL

PISCES, PEGASUS, Alpheratz, ANDROMEDA, AQUILA, TAURUS, Altair, Aldebaran, CYGNUS, Deneb, CASSIOPEIA, PERSEUS, Rigel, LYRA, ORION, Vega, Capella, AURIGA, Betelgeuse, URSA MINOR, Polaris, SAGITTARIUS, Kochab, Sirius, HERCULES, Castor, Pollux, GEMINI, Dubhe, Procyon, Merak, CANIS MAJOR, Antares, SCORPIUS, BOÖTES, URSA MAJOR, Arcturus, VIRGO, LEO, Regulus, Spica

## ORION STEPS ONTO THE SKY
Orion the Hunter climbs into a northern January sky. The three stars of Orion's belt point down to Sirius, the night sky's brightest star, rising through the trees.

## ORION THE HUNTER
In Greek mythology, Orion was the son of Neptune and a great hunter. When Orion boasted that he would hunt down every animal in the world, Gaia, the Earth goddess, sent a scorpion to sting and kill him.

## THE BIG DIPPER
The Big Dipper is a pattern of seven stars in Ursa Major, the Great Bear. In Great Britain, this pattern is known as the Plough. Germans call it the Great Wagon and Three Horses.

### Word Builders

As Earth orbits the Sun each year, the Sun appears to travel through a band of 12 constellations called the **zodiac.** The name comes from the Greek word *zoidiakos,* meaning "circle of animal signs." Seven zodiac constellations are named for animals, such as Cancer the Crab. Four others resemble people, such as Aquarius the Water Bearer. Libra the Scales is the only one that doesn't resemble a living creature.

### That's Amazing!

• On a clear, moonless night far from city lights, the stars seem too many to count. But if you did, you'd count about 2,000 stars that you can see at any moment with just the unaided eye.
• Most constellations are so old that no one knows who named or thought of them. From drawings on clay tablets, we know that 5,000 years ago, Sumerians saw some of the same pictures in the sky that we do today.

### Pathfinder

• Do you need a telescope to see constellations? Go to page 10.
• What are the stars made of? Go to pages 50–51.
• What object can you see in the constellation of Orion? Go to page 55.
• To which galaxy do the constellation stars belong? Go to pages 56–57.

## SOUTHERN SKY STAR CHART

These are the Southern Hemisphere's bright stars, ones you can see from Australia, New Zealand, South America, and southern Africa. Face north and turn the map so the current month is at the bottom. Stars near the horizon are at the edge of the map. Stars overhead and behind you lie toward the map's center.

### HANDS ON
## Following the Stars

When you first look up at the night sky, it can seem overcrowded with stars. Concentrate on the brightest stars, and you'll soon match them up with the charts on these pages.

To identify even more stars and constellations, you can use a planisphere—a round map of the night sky with a top disk that you turn to the current date and time. You can also learn about stars by using a star atlas, a book of detailed star maps. Starmapping computer programs let you print out a map of the night sky for any particular time and place. For your stargazing sessions, dress warmly—you'll be standing still for a long time. Bright lights can ruin your night vision and make it hard to see the stars, so find a dark observing spot and cover your flashlight with red cellophane.

### LEO THE LION
People have seen Leo as a starry lion since ancient times. The six bright stars that look like a backward question mark trace out the lion's head. Leo is one of the 12 constellations of the zodiac.

### SCORPIUS THE SCORPION
Many different people saw Scorpius as a scorpion. In Greek mythology, this is the scorpion that killed Orion. These mortal enemies are opposite each other in the sky—as one rises, the other sets. Scorpius is another zodiac constellation.

# Shining Stars

During the day, you can see one star in the sky—our Sun. At night, with the Sun's glaring light gone from the sky, you can see hundreds of other stars. They are balls of hot hydrogen gas like our Sun, but they are so far away that each appears as a sparkling point of light.

Stars come in many colors and sizes. Our Sun is a yellow star with a surface temperature of 11,000°F (6,000°C). That's hot—but white and blue stars are hotter. Orange and red stars, on the other hand, are cooler. Stars can be average size like our Sun, or they can be giants or dwarfs. If the Sun were the size of a beachball, bright giant stars would be monster balloons as wide as a small town, while dim dwarf stars would be as small as green peas.

A few stars, like the Sun, travel through space alone, but most are multiple stars that are made up of two or more stars dancing about each other. Like the Sun, some stars have families of planets. If you lived on a planet that orbited a multiple star, you would see more than one sun in the sky.

## ALIEN SOLAR SYSTEMS

Astronomers thought other solar systems would look like ours—with small, rocky planets close to a star, and cold gas giants far out. They were surprised to discover solar systems where huge Jupiter-like planets orbit as close to their star as Mercury does to our Sun. Whether these alien solar systems also have small, rocky planets like Earth remains unknown.

## HANDS ON

### Why Stars Twinkle

Do you know why stars twinkle? Try this experiment.

1. Wad up small pieces of aluminum foil to make stars. Place the stars on a piece of dark cardboard.

2. Pour water into a large glass bowl until it is three-quarters full. Place the bowl on top of the silver stars.

3. Make the room dark and shine a flashlight into the bowl.

4. Tap the side of the bowl several times. The water will move, and the stars will look smudged for a moment.

In the same way that the light shining off the foil moves when the water does, starlight passing through Earth's atmosphere travels through layers of moving air that bend the light back and forth. This makes the stars look as if they are twinkling. If you traveled up to the Hubble Space Telescope, beyond Earth's atmosphere, the stars would shine steadily.

## A SHORT HISTORY OF A STAR

Stars are born, live for billions of years, and then die. Throughout their lives, stars change size and temperature as they use up their hydrogen supply. Here is the life cycle of an average star like the Sun.

**A NEBULA COLLAPSES...**
A cloud of gas and dust called a nebula starts shrinking. Squeezed by gravity, its center heats up.

**...A STAR IS BORN...**
The nebula's center becomes so hot that it crushes hydrogen into helium, releasing energy. The star begins to shine.

**...AND LIVES...**
For billions of years, the star is stable, radiating light and heat.

## Word Builders

• Some star names are Greek—**Arcturus** (and the word Arctic) comes from the Greek word *arktos*, meaning "bear." **Sirius,** from the Greek word *Seirios*, means "the brilliant one."
• Other star names are from Arabic words—**Betelgeuse** is from *yad al-jauza*, meaning "the hand of the giant," while **Rigel**, from *rijl*, means "foot."

## That's Amazing!

• An Apollo spacecraft took just three days to travel to the Moon, but it would take 850,000 years to reach the nearest star.
• If you could bring one teaspoon of white dwarf matter to Earth, it would weigh as much as a large truck.

## Pathfinder

• Why are we looking for planets around other stars? Go to pages 18–19.
• What makes the Sun a special star? Go to pages 28–29.
• How can you identify the stars? Go to pages 48–49.
• Which stars end their life with a bang? Go to pages 52–53
• Can you see where stars are born? Go to pages 54–55

## INSIDE STORY

### Planet Hunters

How do you find alien planets? "Just as a leashed dog can jerk its heavier owner around in circles, a planet can swing its star around," explain Paul Butler and Geoff Marcy. The duo were among the first to find planets around other stars. After 10 years of work at  Lick Observatory in California, they detected tiny wobbles in the motions of stars caused by the tug from Jupiter-like planets. The discoveries made them famous. "We got calls from every newspaper, magazine, and TV station there was." The team is now using the Keck and the Anglo-Australian telescopes to hunt for Earth-like planets around 800 nearby stars like the Sun. "Within three to six years," predicts Marcy, "we'll know whether our solar system is special."

**GREAT BALLS OF STARS**
Picture a sky blazing with so many stars that the night is never dark. That's what you'd see from the center of one of our galaxy's globular clusters. Each cluster is a ball of a million ancient stars.

**SPRINKLED STARS**
The Pleiades, or Seven Sisters, are only 50 million years old—so young that the dinosaurs never saw them. They are one of hundreds of young open clusters that are sprinkled around the spiral arms of our galaxy.

**...AND BLOWS OFF GAS...**
The unstable, aging star blows off its outer layers in explosions. The layers turn into a colorful cloud of gas—a planetary nebula—surrounding the star.

**...THEN BALLOONS...**
Eventually, the star's hydrogen fuel begins to run out. It swells to become a red giant star.

**...THEN SHRINKS**
What's left of the star shrinks to the size of Earth. This hot white dwarf will shine for billions more years.

# Changing Stars

OUR SUN SHINES steadily year after year, but not all stars are so stable. Some old stars change size every few days or weeks, becoming brighter as they balloon and dimmer as they shrink. These are known as pulsating variables.

  Other stars change because they belong to double star systems. Some double stars are so close together that one star pulls gas away from the other. The more ravenous star collects enough gas from the other star to set off an explosion known as a nova. After the explosion, the star collects gas again. Some hungry stars collect so much gas that they blow apart as a supernova, one of nature's most powerful explosions. The star is completely destroyed.

  Supernovas can also occur at the end of a giant star's life. Giant stars burn so furiously that they last only a few million years. When their fuel runs out, they explode, crushing their deep core into a neutron star or a black hole. Neutron stars are extremely dense city-size spheres that spin very rapidly. Black holes are infinitely dense and swallow up anything that comes close to them—even light.

## LOOK OUT! THIS STAR'S ABOUT TO BLOW!

Eta Carina is near the end of its life. In 1841, this giant star blew off two puffballs of gas, which have been getting bigger ever since. They are seen here in a 1993 photo from the Hubble Space Telescope. Sometime in the next few thousand years, the star will blow apart as a supernova. When it does, it will look as bright as Venus in our sky.

### INSIDE STORY

## Supernova Watcher

"I was contemplating the stars when I noticed a new star, surpassing all the others in brilliancy, shining directly above my head. I was so astonished at the sight I doubted my own eyes." The new star, discovered by Tycho Brahe in 1572, was a surprise because people thought that stars never changed. By careful observations, Tycho Brahe proved that his supernova lay far beyond the Moon in the realm of the stars. All that remains today of Tycho's star is a gas cloud called a supernova remnant (left). It can be seen only by X-ray telescopes.

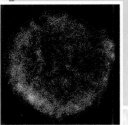

### STARS THAT DANCE

Eclipsing stars revolve around each other as if they are dancing. When one star hides behind the other, its light is cut off, and the pair looks dim in our sky. When the star comes out, the pair looks bright again.

### STARS THAT INFLATE

Every few days or weeks, pulsating stars puff up, cool off, and shrink. Then they heat up and balloon in size again. Astronomers have discovered thousands of these variable stars in the sky. By timing their pulsations, astronomers can calculate how far away the stars are.

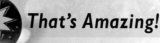

## Word Builders

One eclipsing star that appears to dip up and down in brightness is named **Algol**, from the Arabic word *al-ghul* for "ghoul." In Greek mythology, Algol is the winking eye in the snake-haired head of a woman called the Gorgon. It was thought that anyone who looked at her would turn to stone.

## That's Amazing!

• As they spin, some neutron stars flash pulses of radio beams. When astronomers detect these pulses, they call the star a pulsar.
• A supernova releases as much energy in a few days as the Sun will release in its lifetime of 10 billion years.

## Pathfinder

• How did variable stars expand the universe? Go to page 9.
• Which supernova remnant looks like a crab? Go to page 55.
• Find out more about black holes. Go to pages 58–59.

# SUPERNOVAS

Supernovas are stars that self-destruct, blowing apart in titanic explosions and spewing out clouds of starstuff. Two kinds of stars can explode as supernovas.

## OVERWEIGHT STARS

A blue giant star swells to a red supergiant. The bloated star runs out of fuel in its core. In an instant, the core collapses into a dense neutron star or black hole.

**Stage 1**
Massive blue star

**Stage 2**
Red supergiant star

**Stage 3**
Boom! Supernova explosion

**Stage 4**
Debris expands away from neutron star.

## HUNGRY STARS

The gravity of a white dwarf star sucks gas away from its companion star. The white dwarf becomes too heavy to support itself and collapses. A burst of nuclear fusion tears the hungry star to bits, flinging star debris into space.

**Stage 1**
White dwarf drags material from red giant.

**Stage 2**
White dwarf becomes too heavy.

**Stage 3**
Pow! Supernova explosion

**Stage 4**
Star is destroyed, and star debris blows into space.

### ALL IS QUIET...
It was just an ordinary star, one of millions in a nearby galaxy, the Large Magellanic Cloud.

### ...THEN BANG!
On February 23, 1987, astronomers watched the star explode and become brighter than any supernova since 1604. No one knows when the next supernova will appear.

# Nebulas

THE UNIVERSE CONTAINS more than stars and planets. The space between the stars is sprinkled lightly with atoms of gas and specks of dust. Like water vapor in our atmosphere, some of this starstuff collects into clouds called nebulas. Gravity packs some nebulas so tightly that stars condense from the cool, dark clouds, like raindrops forming in rain clouds.

Once stars form, they become chemical factories. Deep inside their atom-smashing cores, stars turn hydrogen and helium atoms into dozens of other chemical elements. At the ends of their lives, stars blow planetary nebulas and supernova remnants into space. These star-death nebulas carry the elements made inside stars back into space, where they eventually find their way into other nebulas.

Like cosmic recycling plants, these other nebulas, enriched by the stuff from older stars, form new stars, new planets—and new life. The oxygen, carbon, iron, and all the other elements in your body came from stars that lived and died billions of years ago. You are made of starstuff recycled through swirling nebulas.

## INSIDE STORY

### Star Photographer

"We can't hear the stars, nor smell nor taste them, nor can we reach out and touch them. Indeed we can barely see them," explains David Malin as he loads an enormous glass photographic plate. Using the Anglo-Australian Telescope as a giant camera, he's taking a portrait of a nebula so faint the exposure will last an hour or more. Why go to the effort? For Malin, the answer is easy. "Astronomical images are proof of the beauty and endless variety of nature. Photographs are also a tool of discovery. An hour's photography can reveal more than the eye and telescope together can ever see." The photos below of the Trifid and Horsehead nebulas are two of Malin's "cosmic landscapes."

## FOUR TYPES OF NEBULAS
### GLOWING NEBULAS
Bright nebulas are lit up like neon signs by stars deep inside them. The stars' energy makes the gas glow in shades of red, green, and blue. This bright nebula, the Trifid, is 3,500 light-years away. Stars are still forming inside it.

### DARK CLOUDS
Other star-forming nebulas are made of dark, dusty clouds that block the light from distant stars. What shape can you see in this dark nebula? Here's a hint—it's called the Horsehead Nebula.

## Word Builders

**Nebula** is the Latin word for "cloud." When astronomers first used telescopes, any fuzzy patch in the sky that did not look like a star was called a nebula. We now know that many of what the early astronomers called nebulas are not gas clouds in our galaxy. They are really galaxies made up of billions of stars.

## That's Amazing!

• The clouds around the Orion Nebula contain enough gas to make 10,000 Suns.
• Two elements—hydrogen and helium—make up 99 percent of the universe. The other 1 percent—the elements that make planets, living things, and us—first developed inside stars.

## Pathfinder

• Where is the Hubble Space Telescope? Go to pages 10–11.
• How can a nebula turn into a solar system? Go to page 23.
• What sort of star ends up as a planetary nebula? Go to pages 50–51.
• How does a supernova remnant form? Go to page 53.

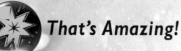

## HANDS ON

### Find the Orion Nebula

The Orion Nebula is a cloud of dusty gas where new stars are forming. The young stars make the nebula glow.

To find the Orion Nebula, start by looking for the constellation of Orion the Hunter, using the star charts on pages 48–49. In the center of Orion is a row of three bright stars, the Hunter's belt. Beneath the belt is the Hunter's sword, made up of three fainter stars.

If you look through binoculars, you'll see that the sword's middle star is much fuzzier than the others. In fact, it is not a star at all—it's the Orion Nebula. In photos the nebula looks red, but through binoculars it looks ghostly gray. That's because our eyes can't see the true colors of stars and nebulas.

## THE EAGLE NEBULA, A STELLAR NURSERY

The Eagle Nebula, 7,000 light-years away, is filled with young stars. A photo taken by David Malin shows the entire nebula (above). The Hubble Space Telescope peered deep into the nebula. Its sharp image (left) reveals pillars of gas and dust towering 1 light-year high. At the tips of the pillars, blobs of gas the size of our solar system contain new stars being born. Our Sun and planets formed out of a similar nebula five billion years ago.

### BLOWING STAR BUBBLES

Dying stars often blow off their outer layers to make bubbles of gas, like this Hourglass Nebula. Because these nebulas looked like dim planets through early telescopes, astronomers named them planetary nebulas.

### STELLAR GRAVEYARDS

The Crab Nebula is what remains of a supernova star that people saw explode in AD 1054. Supernova remnants like the Crab help enrich a new generation of stars.

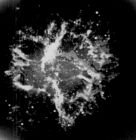

# Our Galaxy

IF THE SOLAR system is your cosmic neighborhood, then the Milky Way galaxy is your sprawling city of stars. This city is made up of 200 billion stars and is so wide that a light beam takes 100,000 years to travel from one side to the other. Star-studded spiral arms spin around the city center, a dense core, or nucleus, that is packed with stars. Our Sun lives in the galactic city's suburbs, in a spiral arm roughly halfway out from the center of the galaxy.

All the stars you see in the sky—every constellation and all the star clusters and nebulas you can see through telescopes— belong to our galaxy. Far away lurks something that you can't see. Using infrared and radio telescopes to probe the center of the Milky Way, astronomers have found stars and gas frantically swirling around a very small, dense, dark object— perhaps a massive black hole.

Just as there are many cities in the world, our galaxy is one of many star-cities in the universe. All the other galaxies are far away—light from the nearest big star-city, the Andromeda galaxy, takes 2.8 million years to reach us.

## YOUR STAR CITY

If you could travel to a place far above the Milky Way, you would see a view like the one shown below—a glowing nucleus of old yellow stars surrounded by a swarm of globular star clusters. Spiral arms studded with young blue stars sweep away from the nucleus. The galaxy would appear motionless because it turns too slowly for human eyes to detect any movement.

Spiral arms

Direction
of rotation

## INSIDE STORY

### Discoverer of Dark Matter

"My earliest recollection," explains American astronomer Vera Rubin, "is of sitting in the back of a car at night and asking my father why the Moon is going where we are going. I can still recall the excitement of the question. Today the excitement I get from asking questions is no less." Vera Rubin's curiosity led her to a remarkable discovery—galaxies are surrounded by clouds of invisible dark matter. Astronomers now think that 90 percent of the matter in the universe is dark, but the identity of the dark matter is a mystery. "Still more mysteries of the universe remain hidden," Rubin says. "Their discovery awaits the adventurous scientists of the future willing to ask some really far-out questions."

## MILK IN THE SKY

In the night sky, we can see the spiral arms of our galaxy. They look like a pale ribbon of light arcing across the sky. We call this hazy band the Milky Way—the same name that we give to our entire galaxy.

## Word Builders

Our galaxy's name, the **Milky Way,** is an English translation of the Latin words *Via Lactea,* meaning "road of milk." The word **galaxy** comes from the Greek word *gala,* meaning "milk." Greek legend tells that the hazy band of light across the night sky was made of milk spilled by the baby Hercules.

## That's Amazing!

• Since the first dinosaurs appeared 228 million years ago, the Sun has made only one orbit of our galaxy.
• At the center of the Milky Way, there might be a black hole that weighs as much as a million Suns.

## Pathfinder

• How does the Milky Way fit into the universe? Go to pages 8–9.
• What did Galileo see when he looked at the Milky Way through a telescope? Go to page 10.

## A GALAXY MENAGERIE

Like animals in a zoo, many kinds of galaxies populate the universe. Most belong to four main species.

**SPIRAL GALAXY**
In spirals like the Whirlpool galaxy, several arms of brilliant stars reach out from a densely packed core. Stars in the arms turn around the core.

**BARRED SPIRAL**
Like the Great Barred Spiral, some galaxies have arms that start from the ends of unusual bars. Our Milky Way galaxy may be a barred spiral.

**ELLIPTICAL GALAXY**
Elliptical galaxies are like cosmic beehives, with billions of stars swarming in every direction. Some elliptical galaxies, such as M87, have grown to monstrous size by devouring other galaxies.

**IRREGULAR GALAXY**
Not all galaxies have tidy shapes. Some are messy collections of stars. The Small Magellanic Cloud is an irregular galaxy that orbits the Milky Way.

### HANDS ON
## Observing the Milky Way

The best place to see the Milky Way is in the country, far from city lights. And the best time is a night near New Moon in summer, autumn, or winter.

If you look at the Milky Way through binoculars, you'll see that it's made up of thousands of stars. In July or August, look for the most crowded part of the band, around the constellation of Sagittarius. Here, you are looking toward the heart of our galaxy. Can you see the dark lanes of dust and gas that cut through the glowing star clouds? These lanes hide the Milky Way's center.

Globular cluster

Nucleus

Possible black hole in center

Sun

**THE DARK SIDE OF THE GALAXY**
From a side view, our galaxy would look like a flying saucer. Stack two CDs on top of each other and stick a marble in the hole, and you have a good scale model of the Milky Way. The galaxy's flat disc and bulging core may be surrounded by a halo of dark matter that we can't see.

# Galaxies and Black Holes

THE UNIVERSE IS like a huge block of Swiss cheese! The 50 billion galaxies in the known universe are not neatly spaced. They clump together into clusters that can contain thousands of galaxies. The clusters bunch into superclusters around bubblelike regions of empty space.

Galaxies are sometimes drawn so close together by one another's gravity that they pull one another out of shape or even collide, triggering bursts of star birth. Large galaxies can even swallow up smaller galaxies. The Milky Way might one day gobble up its neighbors, the Magellanic Clouds.

Every galaxy might contain black holes. Our galaxy alone might have thousands that were created by supernova explosions. But not all black holes are made from single stars. At the center of many galaxies, there are black holes that have swallowed millions of stars. Some galaxies produce such an astonishing amount of energy that they each must have a supermassive black hole at their center. Luckily for us, even the closest black holes are too far away to swallow our Sun.

**POWERHOUSE GALAXIES**
Quasars might be supermassive black holes fed by the densely packed matter in young galaxies. From a region the size of our solar system, a quasar (right) gives off more energy than an entire galaxy.

**COLLIDING GALAXIES**
Galaxies can collide, rip apart, then burst to life with new stars. In the wreckage of the Antennae galaxies' impact (left), billions of young blue stars are starting to shine.

**WHIRLPOOL OF DESTRUCTION**
Journey to the center of a galaxy, and you might find an accretion disc—a whirlpool of stars, gas, and dust spinning around a black hole. The hole itself emits no light, but you can see the radiation given off by the doomed matter as it is torn apart. The hungry hole can't swallow all its food—any gas it doesn't eat shoots away in high-speed jets.

## LOOKING FOR BLACK HOLES

The sharp cameras of the Hubble Space Telescope have peered deep into the centers of other galaxies. While black holes remain hidden, their swirling discs and high-speed jets give them away.

**NGC 4261**
In a galaxy known only by its catalog number, NGC 4261, Hubble captures an image of an accretion disc—the whirlpool around a black hole. You can see hints of a jet shooting from the center of the disc.

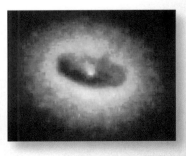

## Word Builders

• As long ago as 1784, English astronomer John Michell realized objects could be so dense that light could not escape from them. But the first person to actually use the words **black hole** was physicist John Wheeler in 1967.
• **Quasar,** coined in 1963, is short for "quasi-stellar radio source."

## That's Amazing!

• If our Sun turned into a black hole (although scientists think it can't), the planets would still orbit it. You must get very close to a hole to be sucked in.
• Crush Earth to the size of a marble, and it would become a black hole.

## Pathfinder

• What instruments are used to find black holes? Go to pages 10–11.
• When can a star turn into a black hole? Go to pages 52–53.
• Why do astronomers think there is a black hole in the center of our galaxy? Go to pages 56–57

## INSIDE STORY

# Down a Black Hole

Oh, no! As you journey through interstellar space, you're falling feet first into a black hole. If you look up, you can see the entire future of the universe flash by in an instant. But the hole is so small that its gravity is pulling on your feet harder than it is on your head. You're being stretched into spaghetti. Ouch! If you had fallen into a bigger black hole, the gravity wouldn't have stretched you quite so much. But some scientists think that the radiation inside any black hole would still get you.

To leap safely across the universe, you'd need to find a wormhole—a cosmic tunnel that connects remote regions of space. Wormholes are popular devices in movies, but no one knows if they really exist. Good luck in your search!

**HEADING TOWARD ANDROMEDA**
Our Milky Way and the Andromeda galaxy are the biggest members of the Local Group, a small cluster of about 30 galaxies. Here you can see Andromeda with its two tiny neighboring galaxies. Andromeda and the Milky Way are speeding toward each other. Five billion years from now, they might collide and form one gigantic elliptical galaxy.

**M87**
A jet of gas that has squirted away from a spinning black hole shoots out of the giant galaxy M87. Its hungry hole has swallowed three billion Suns' worth of starstuff.

**NGC 7052**
In a galaxy 190 million light-years away, Hubble reveals a dusty disc rapidly spinning around a hole 300 million times heavier than our Sun.

**NGC 6251**
The galaxy NGC 6251 is in the constellation of Ursa Minor, the Little Bear. In this Hubble portrait, the white spot is light shining from superhot gas near a black hole in the galaxy.

# The Expanding Universe

DID YOU EVER wonder how our universe began? The Big Bang theory suggests that our universe was born about 15 billion years ago. Though it sounds like science fiction, the theory explains that our universe began when a tiny bubble broke away from another weird universe made of other dimensions, where space and time did not exist. As the bubble broke away, time began. The bubble exploded and grew superhot. As it cooled, it formed all the matter and energy we see today.

The explosion is still happening—we see all the galaxies rushing away from one another. Like a balloon blowing up, space is getting bigger, carrying galaxies farther apart. This expansion of the universe was discovered in the 1920s. Then in the 1960s, cosmic background radiation—the dim heat of the Big Bang—was detected. These are two strong pieces of evidence for the Big Bang theory.

Like all theories, the Big Bang changes with new ideas and new evidence. One idea proposes that our universe may be one of many universes connected together. Another idea, called inflation, suggests that our universe is so enormous that if it were the size of Earth, then the part of the universe we can see would be smaller than a speck of dust. One thing is certain—the universe is filled with so many mysteries, we will never run out of amazing things to discover.

## INSIDE STORY

### Space and Time Mastermind

"I am still trying to understand how the universe works," says Stephen Hawking, speaking through his computer. His body is paralyzed by a muscle disease, but Stephen Hawking has used his mind to explain how space and time began. Explaining the Big Bang, he says it's "a bit like the North Pole of the earth. One could say that the surface of the earth begins at the North Pole." Time itself began in the Big Bang—so just as it makes no sense to ask what is north of the North Pole, it makes no sense to ask what happened before the Big Bang.

## THE BEGINNING OF THE UNIVERSE

A bubble of time and space, searing at a temperature of trillions of trillions of degrees, blows up like a cosmic balloon. As it expands, it cools. Tiny particles called electrons and quarks condense into an atomic soup. The soup congeals to make particles called neutrons and protons. Then atoms of hydrogen and helium form. Gravity clumps these atoms together to form the first stars and galaxies.

**Time = 0 seconds**
Bang! Time and space begin.

**Time = 1 billion trillion trillionth of a second**
Matter (electrons and quarks) forms.

**Time = 300,000 years**
Atoms (hydrogen and helium) form.

**Time = 1 billion years**
First stars and galaxies form.

## WRINKLES IN SPACE

By peering into radiation that has been traveling for billions of years, the Cosmic Background Explorer satellite gazed back in time to 300,000 years after the Big Bang. The blue areas pictured here are cool, lumpy regions of the young universe. Out of these wrinkles, superclusters of galaxies formed.

## Word Builders

The label **Big Bang** was first used in 1950 by Fred Hoyle, who had devised his own Steady State theory of the universe. He was opposed to the Big Bang theory and made up the name to make fun of it. Maybe the name suggested by the Calvin and Hobbes cartoon characters would be better—Horrendous Space Kablooie!

## That's Amazing!

• Just after the Big Bang, in the tiniest fraction of a second, the universe grew 100 trillion trillion trillion trillion times bigger.
• The universe contains roughly as many stars as there are grains of sand on all the beaches of the world.

## Pathfinder

• Who discovered that the universe is expanding? Go to page 9.
• Is there life anywhere else in the universe? Go to pages 18–19.
• How was the solar system born? Go to page 23.
• How are stars created? Go to pages 50–51.

## HANDS ON
### Balloon Universe

You can make your very own universe.

① Blow up a round balloon until it is about as big as an orange, and hold the end so air can't escape.

② With a felt-tip marker, draw about 20 galaxies on the balloon. They can be spirals, ellipticals, and irregulars. Make them about the same distance apart.

③ Look in a mirror and keep blowing up the balloon. Can you see the galaxies moving away from each other?

Like the balloon, the universe is expanding, and all its galaxies are moving farther apart.

**Time = 15 billion years**
Today's universe has 50 billion galaxies.

## THE UNIVERSE'S FATE

Though there are other theories about the beginning of the universe, none explains it as well as the Big Bang theory does. But how will the universe end? Scientists think there are two possibilities. Which is right? New telescopes may provide the answer, or they may reveal evidence that our universe behaves in ways we haven't even imagined yet.

### A BIG CRUNCH?
Just as a ball thrown into the air falls back to Earth, the universe may stop expanding and begin falling back together. Trillions of years from now, all matter and energy may squeeze into a hot "big crunch."

### A UNIVERSE WITHOUT END?
Perhaps there isn't enough matter and gravity to stop the universe expanding. In trillions of years, space may become dark as galaxies collapse into black holes. Then the black holes would dissolve into scattered particles.

# Glossary

**asteroid**  An object made of rock and/or metal that orbits the Sun. Also known as a minor planet. Most asteroids orbit in the asteroid belt between Mars and Jupiter.

**astronomy**  The scientific study of the solar system, our galaxy, and the universe.

**atmosphere**  A layer of gas that surrounds a planet, moon, or star.

**atom**  A tiny bit of matter. An atom is the smallest piece of all the different elements, such as hydrogen, oxygen, and iron. Atoms are made of even smaller particles—electrons, protons, and neutrons.

**aurora**  A colored glow in the sky that occurs when particles from the Sun rain down onto Earth's atmosphere. Also known as the northern or southern lights.

**axis**  An imaginary line through the center of a planet, moon, or star. A planet, moon, or star spins, or rotates, around its axis.

**bacteria**  The simplest forms of life on Earth, made of single cells. Bacteria were perhaps the first forms of life to develop.

**Big Bang theory**  The theory that the universe formed when a tiny bubble of energy exploded about 15 billion years ago.

**billion**  A thousand million. In numerals, it is written as 1,000,000,000.

**black hole**  An infinitely dense object with such powerful gravity that even light cannot escape. A black hole can form when a massive star explodes as a supernova. Supermassive black holes have swallowed millions of stars.

**cluster**  A gathering of stars or galaxies bound together by gravity. Loosely bound groups of several hundred young stars are called open clusters. Tightly bound groups of hundreds of thousands of old stars are called globular clusters. Galaxies form galactic clusters.

**comet**  An object made of dust and ice that orbits the Sun. As a comet nears the Sun, its ice melts and forms tails of dust and gas.

**constellation**  One of the 88 official star patterns seen in the night sky.

**convective zone**  A region within a star where hot material moves up to cooler regions and back down again, much like the movement of boiling water.

**core**  The central region of an object. Earth has a core of nickel and iron. The Sun makes its energy through nuclear fusion in its core.

**crater**  A round scar left on a planet or moon where a comet or asteroid has crashed into it.

**crust**  The outer layer of a rocky planet, moon, or asteroid.

**day**  The time a planet or moon takes to spin around once on its axis.

**eclipse**  When one object passes in front of another, blocking or dimming the other object's light. A solar eclipse occurs when the Moon comes between Earth and the Sun. A lunar eclipse occurs when Earth is between the Sun and the Moon.

**eclipsing star**  A pair of stars that revolve around each other and appear to dim and brighten regularly. When one star moves behind the other, its light is cut off and it looks dim. When the star comes out, it looks bright again.

**galaxy**  A group of billions of stars and nebulas, held together by gravity.

**gas giant**  A large planet made mostly of hydrogen. The solar system's gas giants are Jupiter, Saturn, Uranus, and Neptune.

**gravity**  The force that attracts one object to another. Gravity holds planets and moons in orbit and also holds us on the ground.

**horizon**  The imaginary line in the distance where the ground seems to meet the sky.

**Hubble Space Telescope**  A large telescope that orbits above Earth's atmosphere. The Hubble provides the sharpest pictures of stars and galaxies ever taken.

**infrared energy**  Invisible radiation that travels in slightly longer waves than visible light does. You feel infrared radiation as heat when you are near a fire or heater.

**Kuiper Belt**  A region beyond Pluto where thousands of small icy comets orbit the Sun.

**lava**  Molten rock that comes out of a volcano or through a crack in a planet's or moon's surface.

**light-year**  The distance that a beam of light travels in one year—5.9 million million miles (9.5 million million km).

**Local Group**  A cluster of about 30 galaxies, including our galaxy, the Milky Way.

**lunar**  Associated with the Moon, as in "lunar surface" or "lunar eclipse."

**magnetic field**  The region of space in which an object exerts a magnetic force.

**mantle**  The layer inside a rocky planet beneath the crust and above the core.

**meteor**  The bright streak of light created when a meteoroid enters Earth's atmosphere and burns up. Meteors are often called shooting stars.

**meteorite**  A meteoroid that lands on the surface of a planet or moon.

**meteoroid**  A small rock or piece of metal that travels through space. Larger meteoroids are usually pieces of shattered asteroids. Smaller meteoroids are mostly dust particles shed by comets.

**Milky Way** The galaxy that contains our solar system and all the stars you can see in the night sky. Also, the hazy band of stars that arcs across the sky.

**moon** A natural object that orbits a planet.

**near-Earth asteroid** An asteroid that travels close to the Sun and crosses the orbit of Earth.

**nebula** A cloud of dust and gas in space. A nebula can be bright or dark.

**neutron star** An extremely dense, city-size star that is left when a supernova star explodes.

**nova** An explosion caused when a star collects too much gas from its companion star. After the nova, the star starts collecting gas again.

**nucleus** The core of a comet or galaxy.

**Oort Cloud** A swarm of millions of comets that extends from the Kuiper Belt partway to the nearest star.

**optical telescope** A telescope that collects visible light.

**orbit** The path of an object, such as Earth, as it moves around another object, such as the Sun. Also, to move around another object under the control of its gravity, as in "a planet orbits the Sun."

**phases** The changes in the appearance of an object, such as the Moon, as we see more or less of it lit up by the Sun.

**photosphere** The visible surface of the Sun or another star.

**planet** A big object, such as Mars, that orbits a star, such as the Sun. Because it does not produce its own light like a star does, a planet can be seen only because it reflects sunlight.

**planetary nebula** A cloud of gas formed when a dying star blows off its outer layers.

**poles** Two opposite points on the surface of a spinning planet, moon, or star. The axis of a planet, moon, or star passes through the poles.

**probe** A spacecraft that escapes Earth's gravity and explores the solar system. Probes have been sent to study planets, moons, asteroids, comets, and the Sun.

**pulsar** A neutron star that rotates very fast, sending out regular pulses of radio waves.

**pulsating variable** Stars that change size every few days or weeks, becoming brighter as they balloon and dimmer as they shrink.

**quasar** Short for "quasi-stellar radio source," the core of a distant young galaxy that emits an incredible amount of energy.

**radar astronomy** The study of solar system objects by bouncing radio waves off their surfaces.

**radiation** The process that carries energy through space as waves or particles.

**radiative zone** The deep region of a star that transfers energy to the convective zone.

**radio energy** Invisible radiation that travels in longer waves than infrared light does.

**red giant** A large, cool star in a late stage of its life.

**rocky planet** A small planet made mostly of rock. The solar system's rocky planets are Mercury, Venus, Earth, and Mars.

**satellite** A spacecraft or moon that orbits a larger object. Artificial satellites are sent into orbit around Earth to study Earth and space.

**solar system** A group of planets, comets, asteroids, meteoroids, and dust orbiting a central star. Our solar system is made up of nine planets and countless comets, asteroids, meteoroids, and dust specks orbiting the Sun.

**space** The airless region beyond Earth's atmosphere through which the planets, stars, and galaxies travel.

**space shuttle** A reusable NASA spacecraft that carries people and cargo into orbit around Earth.

**space station** A large artificial satellite that orbits Earth and can be occupied by people for long periods of time.

**spiral galaxy** A large galaxy with several starry arms reaching out from a dense core. It resembles a pinwheel.

**star** A large ball of hydrogen gas that produces light and heat. The Sun is a star.

**supernova** An extremely powerful explosion of a star. Supernovas occur when a giant star runs out of fuel and explodes as a supernova, or when a star collects so much gas from its companion star that it blows apart.

**supernova remnant** The gaseous remains of a star that has exploded as a supernova.

**Trojan asteroids** Two groups of asteroids that orbit the Sun in the same orbit as Jupiter.

**ultraviolet energy** Invisible radiation that travels in slightly shorter waves than visible light does. The Sun's ultraviolet radiation causes sunburn.

**universe** Everything that exists—all the galaxies, black holes, stars, nebulas, moons, planets, comets, asteroids, meteoroids, and dust scattered throughout space.

**white dwarf** A small, very hot star near the end of its life.

**X-ray energy** Invisible radiation that travels in shorter waves than ultraviolet light does.

**year** The time a planet takes to complete one orbit around the Sun.

# Index

## A
Aldebaran, 17
Algol, 53
aliens, 18–19
Andromeda galaxy, 8–9, 59
Antennae galaxy, 58
Arcturus, 51
Ares, 33
Armstrong, Neil, 12
asteroids, 22–23, 34–35
astronauts, 12–15
atmosphere, 15
aurora australis, 29
aurora borealis, 29
auroras, 28–29

## B
barred spiral galaxies, 57
Betelgeuse, 51, 56
Big Bang theory, 60–61
Big Dipper, 8, 48
black holes, 52–53, 58–59
blue stars, 50, 53
Brahe, Tycho, 52
Butler, Paul, 51

## C
Caliban, 41
Callisto, 37
Cassini probe, 16–17, 38, 43
Cat's Eye Nebula, 54
Ceres, 34–35
Charon, 23, 42–43
Clementine probe, 17
Comet Hale-Bopp, 45
Comet Halley, 44–45
Comet Hyakutake, 44
Comet Shoemaker-Levy, 36, 45
Comet Wild, 45
comets, 44–45
constellations, 48–49
Copernicus (crater), 27
Copernicus, Nicolaus, 8, 22
Cosmic Background Explorer satellite, 60
cosmic radiation, 60
Crab Nebula, 55
craters, 27

## D
Dactyl, 35
D'Arrest, Heinrich, 40
Deep Space probe, 34, 44
Deimos, 32
dinosaurs, extinction of, 35

## E
Eagle Nebula, 55
Earth, 8–9, 22–25

eclipses, 29
electrons, 60
elliptical galaxies, 57
Eta Carina, 52–53
ETs, 19
Europa, 18–19, 36–37

## G
Gagarin, Yuri, 12
galaxies, 8–9, 56–59
Galileo (astronomer), 10, 36
Galileo (robot probe), 16–17, 36–37, 43
Galle, Johann, 40
Ganymede, 37–38, 42
Gemini (spacecraft), 12
Geminids, 44
giant stars, 52–53
Giotto probe, 17
Global Surveyor probe, 17, 32–33
Great Barred Spiral galaxy, 57
Great Bear, 48
Great Dark Spot (Neptune), 41
Great Red Spot (Jupiter), 37

## H
Halley's Comet, 44–45
Hawking, Stephen, 60
Herschel, William, 40
Hoba West meteorite, 35
Horsehead Nebula, 54
Hourglass Nebula, 55
Hoyle, Fred, 61
Hubble, Edwin, 9
Hubble Space Telescope, 8–9, 10–11, 54–55, 58–59
Huygens, Christiaan, 38
Huygens probe, 17

## I
Ida, 35
infrared astronomy, 11
International Space Station, 15
Io, 22, 36–37

## J
Jupiter, 22–23, 36–37

## K
Keck telescopes, 11
Kuiper Belt, 42, 44

## L
Large Magellanic Cloud, 53
Leo, 49
Leonids, 44

life, on other planets, 18–19
Lowell, Percival, 18
lunar eclipse, 29
Lunar Prospector probe, 26–27
Luna space probes, 26–27

## M
M13, 19
M33, 60
M83, 60
M87, 57–59
Maat Mons, 30–31
Magellan probe, 16–17, 30–31
Malin, David, 54
Marcy, Geoff, 51
maria, 27
Mars, 18–19, 32–33
Mercury, 22–23, 30–31
meteorites, 34
meteoroids, 34–35
Michell, John, 59
microgravity, 15
Milky Way, 8–9, 56–59
Mimas, 22, 38
Miranda, 22, 41
The Moon, 26–27, 29
Moon-walking, 26
moons, of planets, 22–23, 26–27, 32, 36–38, 41–43
MUSES-C spacecraft, 34–35

## N
nanorover, 34–35
National Aeronautics and Space Administration (NASA), 12
nebulas, 50, 54–55
Neptune, 22–23, 40–41
Nereus, 35
Nergal, 32
neutron stars, 52–53
Newton, Isaac, 10
NGC 604, 54
NGC 4261, 58
NGC 4639, 60
NGC 6251, 59
NGC 7052, 59
night and day, 24–25
1997 XF11 (asteroid), 34
novas, 52

## O
Observer probe, 17
Omega Centauri, 56
Oort Cloud, 44
orange stars, 50
orbits, of planets, 22–23
Orion constellation, 48

Orion Nebula, 55–56
Osiris, 48

## P
Pathfinder probe, 16–17
Perseids, 44
phases, of the Moon, 26–27
Phobos, 22, 32
photography, of stars, 54
Pioneer 10 probe, 17
PKS2349 (quasar), 60
planets, 22–23, 51
Pleiades, 51, 56
Pluto, 22–23, 42–43
Pluto-Kuiper Express, 42–43
probes, 16–17, 26–27, 30, 32–33, 45
pulsars, 53
pulsating variables, 52

## Q
quarks, 60
quasars, 58–59

## R
radio telescopes, 11, 19
RD1, 60
red stars, 50, 53
Rigel, 51
rings, of Saturn, 38–39
robot probes, 16–17, 26–27, 30, 32–33, 45
rockets, 12
Rosetta probe, 44
Rubin, Vera, 56

## S
Sagan, Carl, 17
satellites, 14–15, 29, 60
Saturn, 17, 22–23, 38–39
Saturn V rockets, 12–13
Scorpius, 49
seasons, 25
SETI, 19
Seven Sisters, 51
Shepard, Alan, 12–13
Shoemaker, Carolyn, 45
shooting stars, 34
Sirius, 51
skywatching, 49–50
Small Magellanic Cloud, 57
SOHO, 29
Sojourner probe, 16, 32
Sol, 23
solar eclipse, 29
solar systems, 20–23, 50
Soyuz (spacecraft), 12
space exploration, 8–19
space probes, 16–17, 26–27, 30, 32–33, 45

Orion Nebula, 55–56
Space Shuttle, 12–13
space stations, 14–15
spacesuits, 14–15
spacewalks, 14–15
spiral galaxies, 57
star clusters, 50–53
Stardust probe, 45
stars, 48–54
Stonehenge, 28
The Sun, 22–23, 28–29
sunspots, 29
supernovas, 52–53
Sycorax, 41

## T
telescopes, 10–11
Titan, 17–19, 38
Tombaugh, Clyde, 42
Trifid Nebula, 54
Triton, 41–42
Trojan asteroids, 23, 34
Tsan, 48

## U
UFOs, 18–19
Ulysses probe, 17
universe, 8–9, 46, 60–61
Uranus, 22–23, 40–41
Ursa Major, 48

## V
Venera probes, 30
Venus, 8, 22–23, 30–31
Very Large Array (telescope), 11
Viking I probe, 32–33
volcanoes, on Venus, 30–31
Vostok (spacecraft), 12
Voyager probes, 16–17, 37, 40–41, 43

## W
The War of the Worlds (book), 33
weightlessness, 14–15
Whirlpool galaxy, 57
white dwarfs, 51–53
white stars, 50
World Wide Web, 16
wormholes, 59

## X
X-ray telescopes, 11

## Y
yellow stars, 50

## Z
zero gravity, 14–15
zodiac, 48–49

The publishers would like to thank the following people for their assistance in the preparation of this book: Barbara Bakowski, James Clark, Dina Rubin, and Jennifer Themel. Our special thanks to the following children who feature in the photographs: Michelle Burk, Simon Burk, Amanda Hanani, Mark Humphries, Bianca Laurence, Jeremy Sequeira, Gemma Smith, Amanda Wilson, Max Young.

PICTURE CREDITS (t=top, b=bottom, l=left, r=right, c=center, e=extreme, f=flap, F=Front, C=Cover, B=Back) (AAO=Anglo-Australian Observatory, AAT=Anglo Australian Telescope, APL=Australian Picture Library, ASP=Astronomical Society of the Pacific, TPL=The Photo Library, Sydney, SPL=Science Photo Library.)

AAO 54c (D. Malin), 47cl, 53b, 54br, 55cr, 57cr. AAP Image 12r, 15bl, 17b. AAT 57bcr (D. Malin), 54bl, 57br. Ad-Libitum 12ct, 12cb, 19br, 22b, 24bl, 50l, 61t, 111, 26b, 49r (M. Kaniewski). APL 34c (Woodfin Camp), 42bl. ASP 11tr, 29t, 37bc, 42br, 45br, 56bl. Austral 42c (FOTO). Alan Dyer 20cbr, 28tr, 29tr, 48bl. E.T. Archive 52c. Akira Fujii 8cr, 21ebl, 27r, 29br, 37bl, 45bc, 55tr, 62c. IAC Photo 11cr (D. Malin). Image Select 9r. Mary Evans Picture Library 22tr. David Miller 30cr. NASA 9br, 37cl, 38bl, 52/53c (JPL Photo), 58bc (Leiden Observatory/W. Jaffe), 58bl, 59bc, 59br (STScI), 13r, 25r, 30c, 31r, 33tr, 45bl. Newell Color 6rt, 8cl, 47tl, 55bl. Novosti 13c. The Image Bank 28bl (S. Krongard). TPL 51cr, 59c (J. Chumack), 11bl (T. Craddock), 47tc, 54/55c (I. M. House), 59c (Jodrell Bank), 8bl (Nigel Press), 51cl, 56r (SPL/L. Dodd), 17c, 28/29c (SPL/ ESA), 44br (SPL/G. Garradd), 21tl, 33bc (SPL/D. Hardy), 44bl (SPL/Magrath/Nielsen), 11c (SPL/ Magrath Photography), 8br, 14l, 15c, 19c, 31c, 33tl, 35t, 36bc, 36br, 37cl, 41cr, 41bl, 60br (SPL/ NASA), 11br, 52bl (SPL/Max-Planck-Institute), 34l (SPL/J. Samford), 19t (SPL/Dr. S. Shostak), 60bl (SPL/Dr. R. Stepney), 25tl, 47cr, 55br, 58br (SPL), 41r (SPL/US Geological Survey), 57tr (SPL/US Naval Observatory), 9bl, 26c (World Perspectives), 45cl. Tom Stack & Associates 57c (B. & S. Fletcher),

21br, 41br. UA News Services 34tr (L. Stiles). UC Berkeley 51tr (G. Marcy).

ILLUSTRATION CREDITS
Julian Baum/Wildlife Art Ltd 20cr, 26tr, 26cr, 26bl, 26bc, 26br, 27bl, 27br, 36/37c, 37br, 63tr. Gregory Bridges 32bl. Tom Connell/Wildlife Art Ltd 6br, 6ebr, 7tl, 7tr, 12/13c, 12tl, 12tcl, 12tcr, 12tr,12bl, 12bc, 12br, 13bl, 13bc, 13br, 14/15c, 14tl, 14tr, 14bl, 14bc, 14br, 15tl, 15r, 62br, 63bl, 63bcl, 63bcr. Christer Eriksson 7bl, 7br, 18/19c, 18/19b, 18tl, 18tc, 18tr, 63bel. Chris Forsey 5bc, 32/33c, 32bc, 46etr, 46tr, 46r, 48t, 48bl, 49bl, 49br, 50b, 62bel, 63etr, 63br. Murray Frederick 20ctr, 21tr, 24br, 25bl, 25bc, 25br, 35tr, 35cr, 35br. Lee Gibbons/ Wildlife Art Ltd 21cb, 38/39c, 38r, 38bc, 38br, 39bl, 39br, 47tr, 56/57c, 56tl, 56tr, 56bl,,56br, 57b, 62tr, 62bcl. Ray Grinaway 24tl, 6tl, 28tl, 28tc, 28tr, 28bc, 28br, 30tl, 30tc, 32tl, 34tl, 36tl, 36tc, 38tl, 38tc, 40tl, 40tc, 42tl. David A. Hardy/Wildlife Art Ltd 4tr, 4cr, 4br, 6etr, 7cl, 7cr, 8t, 8tl, 8tc, 9c, 16/17c, 16tl, 16tc, 16tr, 16bl, 16br, 17t, 20tr, 21bl, 22/23c, 22t/b, 23r, 23b, 24/25c, 24cl, 26cl, 27c, 28cl, 30cl, 30bl, 32cl, 36cl, 38l, 40/41c, 40l, 40bl, 40br, 42/43c, 42t, 42l, 43t, 43r, 43bc, 44/45c, 44tl, 44cc, 44tr, 44l, 44c, 46b, 46br, 47bl, 47bc, 47br, 48/49c, 52tl, 52tc 52tr 52bl, 52br, 53t, 54tl, 54tr, 58/59c, 58tl, 58tc, 58tr, 59r, 60/61cb, 60tl, 60tc, 60tr, 60bl, 60br, 61tr, 61br, 62etr, 62tl, 62tc, 62bl, 62bcr, 62ber, 63tel, 63tl, 63br. Robert Hynes 41ctr. Peter Mennim 38c. Oliver Rennert 10/11c. Trevor Ruth 21ct, 36c. Marco Sparaciari 4tcr, 6ctr, 6cbr, 10tl, 10tc, 10tr, 10r, 10bl, 10bc, 10br, 11etr, 11ecr, 11ebr, 20br, 30/31b, 30bc, 32tc, 32br, 32br, 33r, 33r, 33br, 63tcl. Chris Stead 46rc, 50/51c. Kevin Stead 62etl. Cliff Watt 37cr. Tony Wellington 34/35c, 34tc, 34bl, 34br. Rod Westblade 24tc, 29c, 31bl. David Wood 25r, 29cr, 50t.

COVER CREDITS
Ad-Libitum Ffcb, FCbl, FCbr, FCcrt (M. Kaniewski). Tom Connell/ Wildlife Art Ltd BCtl, BCbc, BCbr, FCtl, FCt. Digital Stock FCc. Chris Forsey BCc. Lee Gibbons/ Wildlife Art Ltd Bftl, FCcrb, Ffb. Ray Grinaway Fft. David A. Hardy/ Wildlife Art Ltd Bfcl, Bfcr, Bfbl, Bfbr, Bfeb, BCcl, BCbl, BCtr, FCcr, FCtcl, FCcl, FCbcl, FCber, FCct, Ffct. Stock Photos FCbc.